Navajo Scouts
⊢ During the ⊣
Apache Wars

JOHN LEWIS TAYLOR

Published by The History Press
Charleston, SC
www.historypress.com

Copyright © 2019 by John Lewis Taylor
All rights reserved

First published 2019

Manufactured in the United States

ISBN 9781467141956

Library of Congress Control Number: 2019937043

Notice: The information in this book is true and complete to the best of our knowledge. It is offered without guarantee on the part of the author or The History Press. The author and The History Press disclaim all liability in connection with the use of this book.

All rights reserved. No part of this book may be reproduced or transmitted in any form whatsoever without prior written permission from the publisher except in the case of brief quotations embodied in critical articles and reviews.

Contents

Foreword, by Martin Link ... 5
Acknowledgements ... 7

Chapter 1. Settler Nations' Militaries and the Indian Nations ... 9
Chapter 2. The Navajo Cavalry ... 17
Chapter 3. Navajo Scouts ... 24
Chapter 4. Navajo-Apache Relations ... 26
Chapter 5. Apache Tactics ... 30
Chapter 6. Navajo Scouts Take the Field ... 32
Chapter 7. The Victorio War ... 43
Chapter 8. Nana's Raid ... 53
Chapter 9. The Geronimo War ... 59
Chapter 10. Various Roles of Navajo Scouts ... 80
Chapter 11. Old Scouts ... 90
Chapter 12. Economic Factors ... 96
Chapter 13. Social and Cultural Factors ... 98
Chapter 14. The Legacy of the Navajo Scouts ... 101

Appendix. Famous Scouts ... 109
Notes ... 121
Bibliography ... 131
About the Author ... 143

Foreword

One of the unique aspects in the annals of American warfare is the long and continuous involvement of Native American warriors in our country's wars. And the role of the Navajos in this important piece of American history is a fascinating story focusing on the closing years of the nineteenth century.

That story actually had its beginnings on July 3, 1775, at Cambridge Commons, when General George Washington assumed command of all the forces composing the first army of the thirteen American colonies. As the various units passed in review, there was a company of Stockbridge Indians from Massachusetts, "in feathers, paint and nakedness," commented Washington.

From the early settlement period along the Atlantic seaboard and also in the Spanish conquest in the Southwest, natives served often and effectively as allies of the governments that, ironically, were in the process of conquering their lands and tribes.

Members of various eastern tribes fought in the War of 1812 and the Mexican-American War. Both as scouts and as regular soldiers on both sides of the Civil War, Native Americans fought so well that when Congress enacted legislation reorganizing the federal armed forces for postwar purposes in 1866, it authorized the enlistment of one thousand Native American scouts on the western frontier.

Almost half that number—consisting mainly of Crow, Shoshoni, Pawnee, Arapaho, Sioux and Cheyenne warriors—served throughout the numerous campaigns in the mountains and northern plains during the 1870s and 1880s.

During that same period, campaigns were also undertaken against the several Apache tribes located in the high desert and mountains of the Southwest. Military leaders, including General Crook and General Miles, soon learned that sometimes only an Indian could catch an Indian. Although both commanders used Apache scouts, their major reliance was on the recruitment of Navajos, who knew the area, spoke a similar dialect of the Athabaskan language common to all the Apache tribes and had just returned to their ancestral homeland from four years of enforced captivity in eastern New Mexico.

By 1871, with the completion of Fort Wingate, which then served as the military headquarters for the region encompassing the territories of western New Mexico and eastern Arizona, young Navajos answered the call to military service. A hundred or so actually signed up for service in a company of cavalry, and they not only participated in regular army functions but also policed their own Navajo people, dealing with lawbreakers and livestock rustlers.

But many more, including two women, enlisted as regular troopers or scouts during the dozen years of the violent Apache Wars. Hundreds of Navajos performed to the best of their abilities and, with the experiences gained, went on to be political leaders, medicine men or successful ranchers. However, serving as a scout or trooper was no picnic, and all these Navajo soldiers risked their health, well-being and even their lives in performance of their duties.

If you ever have the opportunity to visit the restored buildings of Fort Apache, in east-central Arizona, be sure to follow the path to the post cemetery. The first headstone you will come upon is the burial of "Navajo Bill," a young Navajo scout who had been killed in action while his unit was assigned to Fort Apache.

—Martin Link

Acknowledgements

I would like to thank two of my professors in the history department at Western Kentucky University, Dr. Jack Thacker and Dr. James Bennet. When I was an undergraduate student there in the late 1960s, they awakened my interest in the history of the American West and the United States military. Without the memory of their mentorship in historical research, I do not think I would have been so bold as to attempt to write this work.

I have had a great deal of help in developing this narrative about Navajo scouts and the role of the Navajo people (Diné) in the story of the Southwest. I would like to thank former library director Mary Ellen Pellington, current director Tammie Moe and the staff at the Octavia Fellin Library in Gallup, New Mexico, for their support in helping me find the necessary resources. The Octavia Fellin Library is a treasure-trove of material on the Southwest and its peoples. I also wish to acknowledge the New Mexico History Museum–Palace of the Governors Photo Archives and its photo curator, Daniel Kosharek. The Navajo Nation Museum; its former archivist, Claendra Begay; and its current archivist, Ben Sorrell, along with the Navajo Nation Library's Linda Curtis, were all an immense help in the gathering of information. Also, thanks to Dr. William Dodge and Martin Link, who read early drafts of the text and made wise comments concerning organization of the chapters. I would also like to extend my appreciation to my sister, Marlane Taylor, who prepared the final draft, and to my wife, Betty, who is a descendent of a Navajo scout.

Chapter 1

SETTLER NATIONS' MILITARIES AND THE INDIAN NATIONS

Since the very beginning of European colonization, the colonial powers used native peoples, either as individuals or as nations, as allies against other colonial settlers or native peoples. European powers soon learned that Native American scouts and soldiers were essential to maintaining their hold on colonial interests in North America.[1] The Spanish in Mexico, and in that part of Mexico that would become the United States after 1848, used forces made up of Indian allies. The Spanish and later the Mexican government of New Mexico launched many campaigns against hostile groups. Historians Rich Hendricks and John P. Wilson noted that the typical force sent into hostile territory was made up of fifty to sixty regular troops, thirty to forty local militiamen and three hundred Pueblo auxiliaries. During the Spanish and Mexican period in New Mexico, it was not uncommon for 60 to 75 percent of an army to consist of Indian allies.[2] In some cases, Navajos were used against anti-Spanish Apaches. In 1788, Colonel Don Fernando De La Concha, who was also serving as governor, gathered a force at Laguna Pueblo. He requested help from Navajos and had so many volunteers that he had to send all but a score home. De La Concha wrote, "I dismissed a part of them, thanking them for their good will and presenting them with gifts. I kept, the governor noted, the well known Antonio el Pinto, and nineteen of his family group which is composed of some of the most vigorous individuals and best acquainted with the territory."[3]

During its struggle for independence from England, the American colonies continued the use of native combatants. Beginning in 1775, the American army used native peoples in its ranks; however, the military rarely allowed native peoples to serve as members of the regular United States forces.

There were exceptions. David Moniac, a member of the Creek Nation from Mississippi Territory, graduated from the United States Military Academy at West Point in June 1822, receiving a commission as second lieutenant in the Sixth United States Infantry. He resigned his commission in December of that year and returned to his plantation in Alabama. In November 1836, Moniac returned to active duty, was promoted to major and was given command of a unit of Creek volunteers.

Major Moniac was killed in action while leading his Creek troops in a frontal assault on the Seminoles at the Battle of Wahoo Swamp, in today's Sumter County, Florida.[4]

When the Civil War began, many American Indians chose to take part. Those who supported the United States were enlisted as home guards or scouts in volunteer units, serving along the western border lands and the Indian Territory.[5] In the more populated states of the North, American Indians had to overcome racist restrictions and the legal fact that they were not United States citizens. It was not until 1862 when many Indians were allowed to serve in Union volunteer regiments. One such unit was the 132nd New York State Volunteer Infantry, D Company, which was made up of members of the Iroquois Nation.[6]

For a Native American to become an officer in the regular United States Army, it was more difficult than serving in a volunteer regiment. In 1861, Ely Parker, citizen of the Iroquois Nation, offered to raise a regiment of Iroquois volunteers to serve the Union cause. He was told by Edwin D. Morgan, the governor of New York, that Indians were not wanted in the New York Volunteers. Parker then offered his service to the Federal government as an engineer. Parker was refused again, by Secretary of War William Seward, who informed Parker that "the fight must be settled by white men alone. Go home and cultivate your farm," Seward said, "we will settle our troubles without Indian aid."[7] Ely Parker was more successful in 1863, when General Ulysses S. Grant arranged to have Parker commissioned as breveted captain of engineers in the regular army. Later in the war, Parker was promoted to lieutenant colonel and became Grant's personal military secretary. In this role, he prepared the articles of surrender at Appomattox. He stayed on Grant's staff until 1869, eventually rising to the rank of brigadier general.[8]

At the end of the Civil War, a few natives who had served in volunteer units in the Union army received commissions in the regular U.S. Army. Cornelius C. Cusick, a Tuscarora from New York, was commissioned a

Ely Parker, the first Native American to serve as commissioner of Indian affairs during the Grant administration. *Courtesy of Wikimedia Commons.*

second lieutenant in the Thirteenth U.S. Infantry in June 1866. Eight months later, he was reassigned to the Thirty-First Infantry and sent to the Dakota Territory to serve under General Nelson Miles in the Sioux Wars.[9] Donald McIntosh, an Iroquois citizen, served as a general's clerk during the Civil War. In 1867, he was appointed as second lieutenant, Seventh Cavalry. By 1870, he had been promoted to first lieutenant and was assigned to Fort Abraham Lincoln. On June 25, 1876, Lieutenant McIntosh was killed leading Company G at the Battle of the Little Big Horn.[10]

Navajo Scouts During the Apache Wars

At the end of the Civil War, the United States Congress looked to the future, and many felt that the future was west of the Mississippi. Vast areas of land needed to be opened to settlement, a task made easier by the completion of the transcontinental railroad in 1869. At the same time, the large army and navy, made up of volunteers who had served during the Civil War, were disbanded and the soldiers and sailors sent home. The postwar military was to have two major missions: the occupation and reconstruction of the former Confederacy and the extension of United States sovereignty across the continent.[11] The function of the post–Civil War army would be different from that of the volunteer and conscript force raised to save the Union. Much of the army's effort in the West was to be spent not only protecting settlers but also protecting Indian lands against trespass by white squatters. In many places, the army was responsible for issuing rations and treaty goods to reservation Indians. The military also played a role in the politics of the Western Territories by overseeing civil elections, controlling the whiskey trade and pursuing and arresting criminals. The military provided labor to improve roads and trails and build forts and camps. The primary intent of this new military was to perform "public works" on behalf of the American people and not to combat Indian resistance to American settlement.[12] The new frontier army was to be as self-sufficient as possible. Where climate and rainfall allowed, the men planted and worked large gardens where they raised fresh vegetables and fruits. The troops also cared for cattle, sheep, chickens and other livestock.[13]

The postwar military was not to be an army of conscripts and state volunteers who served during the Civil War but rather an army of professional officers and enlistees. The officers, for the most part, were West Point graduates, while the enlisted men were made up of men seeking adventure, security, anonymity, social mobility or survival in a new country. A large portion of the enlistees comprised recent immigrants from Europe. Military enlistments rose or fell with the economy of the nation. The pay for the soldiers was low, but it was better than many of the enlistees could make in civilian life.[14]

To meet the military needs of the postwar era, on July 28, 1866, the 39th Congress of the United States passed *An Act to Increase and Fix Military Peace Establishment of the United States*, more popularly known as the "Army Reorganization Act." A major provision of this act was the creation of four additional regiments of cavalry and eight companies of infantry to be made up of colored enlisted men and white officers. This provision created the Buffalo Soldiers, a recognition of the contributions made by the thousands of black soldiers to the Union victory.[15] Also, Section Six of the "Army Reorganization Act" authorized the army to enlist up to one thousand Native Americans to act as scouts and receive the pay and allowances of regular U.S. troops. The Indian scouts were to serve six-month tours of duty, with the option to reenlist if they wished. Many did so and formed a core group of enlistees that played an important role in campaigns against hostile Indians across the West.[16]

By the 1850s, policy makers in the federal government felt that the only practical and humane answer to the "Indian Problem" was to assimilate them into Anglo-American culture. Failure to assimilate would lead to either death or a parasitical existence on reservations.[17] Army officers often presented military service as a means of assimilating the Native American into white society.[18]

While touring the West in 1860, the British traveler and ethnographer Captain Richard Burton concluded that the U.S. Army should imitate the British in India by raising native regiments. Officers he talked to agreed, but they judged that the public's fear of atrocities that might be committed by the "savages" would block such a measure.[19]

The army act of 1866 regularized the practice of Indian-military cooperation by making it possible to integrate Indians into the regular army establishment. Commanders in widely separated areas of the West found the Indians' service so useful that they begged for authority to enlist more. There could be no more eloquent testimony to the scouts' value than the appeals for their services by hard-pressed department commanders.[20]

In September 1880, Captain H.C. Cushing wrote an article in the military magazine *United Service* titled "Military Colonization of Indians." Cushing recommended that entire Indian bands be inducted into military service using the model by which the ancient Romans assimilated the Germanic tribes. Cushing said that the Indian could not become Christian farmers in a sudden transformation, but with the guidance of officers selected for their proven ability to work with Indians, the process could be accelerated.[21]

General George Cook wrote, "The mere fact that scouts were subject to rules and regulations was bound to have a good effect." Cook believed that military service would lead to acculturation through imitation and that acculturation would one day lead to citizenship and enfranchisement. The "Indian Problem" would be solved by assimilation into American society.[22]

The prospect of Native Americans serving in the military did not have universal support within the army. General Philip Sheridan questioned the idea of enlisting large numbers of scouts, feeling that by doing so it would hurt the esprit de corps of the army. Sheridan was also unsure if scouts would remain loyal if they had to serve against their fellow tribesmen. An article in the *Army Navy Journal* warned that Rome had fallen in part because of its reliance on barbaric mercenaries and that the use of Indians in the military would eventually undermine the moral fiber of America. "Indians," the author wrote, "simply don't have the patriotic instincts a soldier must have."[23]

There were also many objections that came from outside the military. In May 1871, President Grant appointed Vincent Colyer, of the Board of Indian Commissioners, to survey the status of Indians in the West. Colyer was given the authority to locate tribes on suitable reservations and to bring them under the control of the proper officers of the Indian Bureau. He felt that war was a futile method of Indian control and that only a policy of peace and assimilation could result in success.[24] Therefore, he disapproved of enlisting Indian scouts, as he thought it disgraceful to take "peaceable Indians from cornfields…[c]ompelling them to go on the warpath against their brethren."[25] Other reformers felt that army life would introduce Indian recruits to alcohol and gambling and that army forts located in Indian country would lead to a degeneration of morals among the Indian peoples.[26] Nonetheless, the ultimate aims of the army, the Indian Bureau and the Christian reformers were the same: to subject the Indian completely to white authority and to make them live in a way acceptable to white prejudice.[27]

American Indians enlisted in the military for various reasons. Some hoped for personal gain, regular rations, clothing and a cash income. Others had in mind a long-term strategy for the benefit of their family, clan and tribe. Their purposes for serving were not necessarily those imagined by whites. For instance, the Indians often acted on the notion that whites could be used to serve Indian purposes. Many looked on military service as an education in finding out the ways of the white man and as a way of finding much-needed activity and self-respect.[28]

Scouts and their families were entitled to other benefits, such as finding work at the forts and medical care from the post infirmary. John Rope, a Western Apache who enlisted at San Carlos Reservation, was delighted because his spouse, as well as the other scouts' wives, was allowed to draw out five dollars per month worth of supplies from the commissary at Fort Thomas.[29]

Army service also afforded men, many of whom took great pride in their personal courage and martial skills, an opportunity and the means to demonstrate their valor and military prowess. Service in the army thus

Navajo Scouts During the Apache Wars

Navajo Indian scout and family. Scouts' families often lived with them on or near military posts. *Courtesy of Hayden Labriola, Arizona State University, Tempe, Arizona, S138:1 #18898.*

enabled an Indian scout to regain his self-esteem. Nonetheless, it should also be remembered what historian David Smitts has pointed out:

> *No treatment of Indian motives for rendering assistance to the frontier army would be complete without the recognition of a crucial but generally ignored historical fact: The frontier army often employed coercion to obtain compliance from so-called friendlies. To be sure friendlies longed for a return to the warrior's life, and there were many instances when Indians were more than willing to help the army defeat old tribal enemies. But the army commanders also commonly relied on intimidation, compulsion, the offer of bribes, and on the abject dependence of reservation Indians to acquire their services. The army's strong-arm tactics are not surprising. Commissioned and noncommissioned officers, generally sought to win unquestioning obedience to orders by instilling in the white private soldier fear of the punishment for disobedience. No Indian would have been considered deserving of less drastic measures to obtain compliance.*[30]

The army gave many Indian men their first real introduction to the culture that would soon dominate their lives. Military service may have simply provided them with a mode of assimilation congenial to their inclinations, their talents and their self-respect.[31]

Indian scouts were organized into companies of twenty-five men under the command of a white officer and a noncommissioned officer. In some cases, the officer in charge was a civilian chief of scouts. At first, most noncommissioned officers were not Indian, but as time went by more Indians filled this role. Coso Meho, as well as other Navajo scouts, became NCOs during their service.[32]

Indian scouts were issued regulation firearms, for the most part the 1873 Springfield Trapdoor rifle or the Springfield Trapdoor carbine. Scouts also received a canvas-covered leather cartridge belt with loops to hold fifty .45-70 cartridges required for the Springfields.[33] Uniforms were the standard blue enlisted man's blouse and trousers. However, most scouts preferred native garb in the field. Navajo scout "War Boy" said, "The army was quite generous with its clothing, but the Navajos didn't want it. It was too tight, and for that reason a person couldn't run fast enough. That is why they didn't want it."[34]

The primary military role of the Indian scout was to locate the enemy, determine its strength, guide troops to its position, make a silent approach and attack.[35]

Besides scouting and guiding troops and civilians, Indian scouts also interpreted and translated; carried dispatches and mail; served as "secret service" agents (i.e., spying and acting as provocateurs); trailing; "peace talking" (i.e., encouraging surrender); hunting; providing escorts for hunting parties of prominent men, for paymasters, for scientific expeditions and for visitors to Indian country; patrolling the railroad lines; guarding railroad construction crews and surveyors; identifying unknown Indians; engaging in combat with hostiles (either independently or together with troops); performing guard duty at picket stations and military posts; helping to keep order on the reservations when Indian police were unable to handle disturbances; chasing army deserters; and more. In 1909, for example, scouts on the Fort Sill Reservation were actually converted to truant officers.[36]

Civilian scout James Cook listed the traits of the ideal Indian scout: loyalty, superior endurance, a good sense of direction and common sense.[37]

It should be noted that Indian scouts were unquestionably essential supplements of the frontier army in its struggles against hostile Indians in the late nineteenth century. They performed beyond the army's highest expectations, routinely exceeding the achievements of white regular soldiers.[38]

Chapter 2

THE NAVAJO CAVALRY

The Navajo War of 1863–64 left the Navajo country in ruins. Conflict between the United States and the Navajos began almost as soon as General Stephen Watts Kearny's Army of the West entered New Mexico on August 18, 1846. One of Kearny's first actions was to reassure the New Mexicans that the United States would "protect the persons and property of all quiet and peaceable inhabitants within its [New Mexico's] boundaries against their enemies: the Eutaws [Utes], the Navajo, and others."[39] This statement joined the United States in the century-old conflict between the New Mexicans and the Pueblo Indians and the Navajos. It was a declaration of war against the Navajos. In September 1846, a United States dragoon noted in his journal that New Mexicans and Pueblo Indians were raising loud complaints against the Navajos taking their livestock, and in October, General Kearny authorized New Mexicans in the Rio Abajo region (south of Albuquerque) to form "war parties" against the Navajos, who were raiding in that region. Expeditions against the Navajos by New Mexicans and their Pueblo allies were a part of New Mexico life. The objectives of the expeditions were to recover stolen livestock, free captives, steal new livestock and capture Navajo women and children as slaves. The slave trade in New Mexico was a major cause of the conflict between the various tribes and the New Mexicans. In November, American military leaders met with several Navajo leaders at Ojo Del Oso (Shash bi Toh, or Bear Springs, the future site of Fort Wingate) and were told by Navajo leader Sarcillos Largo that the Americans should not interfere with their war against the New Mexicans.

NAVAJO SCOUTS DURING THE APACHE WARS

Navajos under guard at Hwéeldi, aka Bosque Redondo. *U.S. Army Signal Corps, courtesy of Place of the Governors Photo Archive, New Mexico History Museum (NMHM/DCS), #028534.*

The conflict increased until, in the 1860s, the United States military launched a scorched-earth campaign against the Navajos.[40]

By 1864, many if not most Navajos had been forcibly relocated to Bosque Redondo (Hwéeldi) on the Pecos River near Fort Sumner, New Mexico, some three hundred miles from Diné Bikéyah, the Navajo homeland. In June 1868, after signing a treaty of peace with the United States, the Navajos were allowed to return home.

When the Navajos returned from Fort Sumner in 1868, they found their fields weed-grown, corrals and hogans destroyed and water sources silted up. In addition to a devastated homeland, the promised rations, tools and replacement livestock from the United States Indian Bureau did not arrive on time.[41] Nature itself added to the unrest because the early 1870s was a period of frequent drought and early freezes that hampered food production.

These conditions during the early 1870s made another Navajo War seem likely, a war that neither the Navajo leadership nor the United States government wanted. Each side felt that it could not afford another Bosque Redondo. In 1870, W.F.M. Arny, ex-governor of New Mexico Territory and now special Indian agent for the territory, reported that the Navajos were restless and bands of Navajos were leaving the reservation to raid and steal livestock from Hispanic and Anglo ranchers. Arny feared that if something were not done, a war with the Navajos would result.[42]

Navajo Church (now called Church Rock) near Fort Wingate. *John K. Hillers, courtesy of Place of the Governors Photo Archive, New Mexico History Museum (NMHM/DCS), #112990.*

In the spring of 1872, the *Santa Fe New Mexican* reported that Navajo raiders had run off five hundred head of sheep from the Rio Puerco Oriental Valley. In July, Navajos appeared near Las Vegas and Fort Union stealing several head of horses and cattle from local ranches.

Navajo agent John Miller reported to Washington that unless the Navajos were issued more corn and beef rations, it would be "utterly impossible to prevent them from going off the reservation in large bodies to commit depredations on citizens."[43]

Navajo leader Manuelito worked to restore harmony by returning stolen animals to the agency at Fort Defiance. He knew that a return to raiding, no matter what the cause, would lead to war. The Bosque Redondo experience had taught the Navajo leadership that warfare and raiding were no longer practical.[44]

In general, the raiding increased as the conditions declined. To deal with the problem, General Oliver O. Howard, special Indian commissioner, was sent in July 1872 to New Mexico Territory. After a stop in Santa Fe to purchase horses and supplies, he proceeded on to Fort Wingate in the company of Major Nathaniel Poe, New Mexico superintendent of Indian affairs, and Reverend David McFarland, a Presbyterian missionary. Howard's reason for visiting New Mexico was to meet with Apache and Navajo leaders and settle all the problems that had developed, including raiding and hostilities between the two tribes. After a shaky start, the Apache-Navajo conference went well enough, and the two tribes agreed to live in peace.

General Oliver O. Howard, Civil War general, head of the Freemen's Bureau and special Indian affairs commissioner for the Grant administration. *Courtesy of Library of Congress, Washington, D.C., #LC-US 262-100786.*

On August 4, Howard met with Manuelito and other Navajo leaders to discuss the problems between the Navajos and New Mexico ranchers. Howard viewed Navajo raids as a "crying evil along the borders of the great Navajo reserve." "Frontier stockmen," Howard said, "were accustomed to use vast stretches of unoccupied public domain for pasturage. Naturally, they lost a great deal of stock and right or wrong accused the Indians."[45]

During the negotiations, Manuelito proposed that the Navajos would regulate thieving themselves and return all stolen livestock to the "Mexican settlements on the Rio Grande."[46]

Having a Navajo patrol was not a new idea. John C. Lowrie, secretary for the Presbyterian Board of Foreign Missions, had previously proposed this idea to Columbus Delano, the secretary of interior. Lowrie wondered why Indian policemen could not be used instead of white soldiers. Lowrie felt that soldiers posted on or near Indian lands were a corrupting influence

Navajo leader Manuelito. *Ben Wittick, courtesy of Place of the Governors Photo Archive, New Mexico History Museum (NMHM/DCS), #0152329.*

on the Indians, introducing alcohol and luring the local women into prostitution. Lowrie used as an example the British colonial government's use of native troops in India, who were, he said, excellent soldiers. Besides, Lowrie reasoned, the military life of drill and discipline would have a civilizing effect on the native population.[47] In addition to Lowrie's proposal, several agents to the Navajos had explored this idea, but none was able to gain approval and funding.[48] The deciding factor was the support of Navajo leaders for the creation of a Navajo force to control lawlessness within their own nation.

Using these previous recommendations as support, General Howard issued a directive to Major Pope to "make the experiment of a small police force in charge of Manuelito the war chief." Major Pope requested special agent to the Navajos Thomas V. Keam to recruit a company of Navajo cavalry made up of one hundred Navajos selected from the various Navajo bands, with this force to be led by Manuelito. Manuelito requested that the Navajo cavalry be dressed in United States Army uniforms so that they would be respected by both whites and Indians.[49]

Before the end of 1872, Manuelito and Keam had recruited ninety-nine Navajos to join the cavalry with a pay of five dollars per month. Manuelito commanded the scout force at forty-eight dollars per month. The Navajo leadership was ready to show that they wanted peace and that the Navajos could keep order among their own people better than the United States military.[50]

To ensure full support, cavalry membership was drawn from each of the various Navajo bands. Each Navajo cavalryman was to provide his own mount. Agent Pope planned to arm the Navajo cavalry with surplus carbines from the Fort Union arsenal, but the War Department turned down the request. The weapons were provided by the Indian Bureau. A shipment of one hundred carbines, slings and cartridges was delivered to Fort Wingate in October 1872.

Paying the Navajo cavalry was a problem. Agent Keam noted on September 9, 1872, that the police force had not been paid, nor had they received any clothing as promised in August. Keam said that the Navajos were making "anxious inquiries" about the lack of action by the Indian Bureau and the military.

Despite the problems of payment and the late issue of supplies, the Navajo cavalry proved to be effective in controlling raiding. In June 1872, Navajo cavalrymen returned stolen horses and other stock taken from Abiquiu and Tierra Amarilla, as well as other settlements in the Rio Grande Valley.

Navajo Scouts During the Apache Wars

Navajo police, 1930s. *Courtesy of Betty E. Taylor.*

In December 1872, W.F.M. Arny stated that due to the success of the Navajo cavalry, a native police force should be established on all the reservations of the "wild tribes" and that this force should be paid.[51]

The Navajo cavalry was successful but proved to be too costly. By September 1873, the unit had been terminated due to lack of funding by Congress. Although active for only thirteen months, the Navajo cavalry became the prototype for the Navajo Indian scouts and, later, the Navajo police force.

Chapter 3

NAVAJO SCOUTS

On January 23, 1873, the secretary of war authorized the Military District of New Mexico to enlist fifty Indian scouts, but Navajos had served in the military before 1873. In February 1861, Captain E.R.S. Canby noted that he had sent two Navajos as scouts, wearing distinctive markings showing that they were in the service of the United States, when they were fired upon by a party of New Mexican raiders from Jemez. One of the scouts, Canby said, was killed and scalped.[52]

At Fort Sumner, several Navajos were enlisted into the military as scouts; these Navajo were known as Red Coats. Their mission was to return to the Navajo Nation and persuade Navajos hiding from the army to give up and return with them to Fort Sumner, where they would be given food and be safe from raiding New Mexicans and Utes. Frank Apache, in a 1969 taped interview, tells the story that his people were hiding near Mount Taylor in New Mexico when they met some Red Coats, who told them that they were trying to help their people and that they should go with them to Fort Sumner, where there were all kinds of good things to eat. Frank Apache's grandfather, who was the leader of the group, told the people that the Red Coats seemed like good people and went with them to Fort Defiance and later to Fort Sumner. Frank Apache said when he got to Fort Sumner, he joined the Red Coats and went with the soldiers to help them find more Navajos. Frank said, "I was enlisted into the army and given a uniform and dress-up like a solider and given a horse. This is the way a joined the army." Frank pointed out that the soldiers found it hard to find the Navajos, but the

Red Coats knew where they lived, so wherever they went they were able to bring several back to Fort Defiance until there were enough to go to Fort Sumner. The Red Coats, Frank said, kept looking for groups of Navajos until it was time to come back from Fort Sumner, around 1868.[53]

In March, Major William Redwood Price at Fort Wingate had enlisted ten Navajos to serve. In Price's view, and that of other military leaders in New Mexico, the support of Navajos was needed to deal with the hostile tribes. Navajos knew all the hiding places in the vast region of canyons and mountains of Apacheria and were recognized for their ability as trackers. In 1871, before the authorization to enlist scouts, Major Price took Troops E and K of the Eighth Cavalry and fifteen Navajos serving as contract scouts to Camp (later Fort) Apache at the request of Colonel John Green, commander of Camp Apache. However, the ten scouts enlisted in 1873 were the first Navajos to serve as regular members of the U.S. Army. Indian scouts were paid the same as all troops, thirteen dollars per month, as well as an extra forty cents per day if they provided their own horses.[54]

Navajo leader Mariano supported Navajos enlisting in the army. He feared that if the Navajos did not serve in the scouts, they would be forced out of non-reservation lands. He also thought that if Navajos were in the army, it would give the tribe an advantage in dealing with the government.[55] Navajo leader Manuelito did not fully agree with Mariano. He wanted Navajos to serve as noncombatants, not wanting to risk any chance for further conflict. Mariano was able to argue his case before a tribal meeting, and his view prevailed.[56]

Navajo historian Jennifer Nez Denetdale wondered why Navajo men would join a branch of the United States military so soon after the Long Walk. For an answer, she looked to the military history of her own great-great-grandfather Dagha Ch'ii, who served in the Navajo cavalry and as a scout in the Apache Wars. Dr. Denetdale's conclusion was that Navajo men served first to support their families and secondly to help resolve tensions between Navajos and the United States. Additionally, the Navajos always feared that any conflict with Indians would sooner or later be blamed on the Navajos, and consequently, they might be again imprisoned.[57]

Chapter 4

NAVAJO-APACHE RELATIONS

The Navajos and Apaches shared a common Athabaskan heritage of a related language family and spiritual beliefs. On the basis of these relationships, anthropologists have divided the Apacheans into seven major communities: the Jicarillas, Lipans, Mescaleros, Chiricahuas, Navajos, Kiowa-Apaches and Western Apaches. However, related cultural backgrounds did not make for a peaceful relationship between the two groups since both peoples were dependent on a "raid and trade" economy.

Apaches often raided Navajo ranches, carrying off livestock and slaves. The Navajos also took part in raids on Apache ranches, taking slaves as well as anything of value. The Navajos were less dependent due to their extensive farming practices and more settled life, following their herds but staying within a boundary based on extended family usage. The Apaches were more nomadic and farmed only on a small scale. The Apache farming system was based on seasons, planting in the spring and returning in the fall to harvest. The rest of the year, the Apaches were almost constantly on the move.[58]

According to historian Grenville Goodwin, Anna Price, a White Mountain Apache, recalled a Navajo attack at Turkey Creek near Fort Apache. A party of three Apache boys was out hunting when the boys were attacked by Navajo raiders. One of the boys was killed, but the other two escaped to spread the news. Apache leader Diablo called for a retaliatory raid against the Navajos; after the proper rituals, a war party was sent out. Diablo's scouts soon picked up the Navajos' trail and followed it into the Navajo Country.

Navajo family, 1880s. *Courtesy of Wikimedia Commons.*

At first, they found the Navajos had moved, as Anna recounted:

> *When they killed the Apache boy they knew we would be attacked by our people.* [The next day the war party found the new Navajo camp and at dawn attacked.] *All at once, the men rushed among the Navajo camp and began killing them. The Navajos rushed out of the camp*

and formed a line to allow their women and children to escape. The fight lasted a short time and no Apache was killed. After the fight was over they [Apache raiders] and took to all they had-bridles, bits, silver, blankets. The men who had come on foot got horses and rode off with Navajo saddles and Navajo blankets tied behind. The war party returned home very fast because they knew that the Navajos would be after them.[59]

Naajebaaye, the daughter of White Mountain Apache leader Hashkeedasilla, told about a time when some Navajos came to trade with her people but slipped back at night and stole some cattle. The Apaches went after them and, after a short running fight, recovered the stolen cattle.[60]

The Apaches also raided Navajo ranches before and after the Navajos returned from Fort Sumner. Most of these raids have gone unrecorded except in oral history. One raid that is remembered was in June 1878, when twenty Apaches attacked two Navajo communities located on the northern edge of the Painted Desert. In their pursuit, the Navajos lost the trail of the Apaches, but a group led by two young men, B'ugoettin and Bahe, was able to cut off the Apaches and catch them at a cave in Diablo Canyon. After a fierce fight, the Navajos killed the Apache raiders and recovered all the stolen property.[61]

The fact that some Apache groups helped the army in the Navajo campaign (September 1863–January 1864) did not build good feeling. Palmer Valor, a White Mountain Apache, recalled that they were told that all the White Mountain people were to go on the warpath against the Navajos and that they were to meet the soldiers at a certain place and help them against the Navajos. Valor said that about two hundred Apaches enlisted, but not like scouts. "We were on our own and only helping the soldiers who we were to join."[62]

Placing the Navajos and Mescalero Apaches together at Bosque Redondo also led to bitterness. Lozen, Victorio's sister, said that at Bosque Redondo Navajos and Apaches alike suffered from hunger and disease, but they fought like dogs among themselves.[63] John C. Cremony, a military officer, reported conflict between the Apaches and Navajos at Bosque Redondo, including a raid on the Apache horse herd by Navajos.[64] In his 1872 report, Vincent Colyer of the Board of Indian Commissioners observed that the only enemies of the Apaches besides the Mexicans were the Utes and the Navajos.[65]

Big Mouth, a Mescalero Apache, said of the years at Bosque Redondo, "That life got much worse when the soldiers brought in many Navajos, maybe nine thousand, and put them above the Pecos River from the four hundred Mescaleros settled there. The Navajos were our enemies and they fought with us and stole our horses and cattle."[66]

Not all relations between the two people were antagonistic. Navajos and Apaches traded, and there was a degree of intermarrying. Mangas Colorado sought to build an alliance with Navajos by the marriage of one of his daughters to a principal Navajo leader.[67] The Apache wife of Mariano, the Navajo leader who helped to organize the Navajo scouts, was the aunt of two wives of the Ojo Caliente leader, Loco.[68]

Sometimes the two groups helped each other in times of conflict with others. Frank Goldtooth told how his grandmother and her family walked to join the Chiricahua Apaches during the Navajo War and remained with them until the Navajos returned from Fort Sumner. Frank's grandmother told him that the Apaches gave her several goats that she used to restore her livestock herd when the family returned to Navajo country.[69]

Chapter 5

APACHE TACTICS

The Union volunteer army that fought the Civil War had been disbanded by 1868, but many of the officers had remained in the military and were now serving in the Southwest. In the Southwest, they had a new enemy—one that required different tactics than those they had learned at West Point and which had proven to be successful against the Confederates. Officers would spend years learning the Apache method of warfare, and they found that Apache success was built on certain basic goals and procedures. The goal of the Apache war leader was to inflict the maximum amount of damage on the enemy with the minimum amount of loss.[70] At the core of the Apache battle plan was the raid. Apaches maintained that there were two types of raids: the Spoils Raid, a key component of the Apache economy where a raiding party hoped to gain as much loot from an enemy as it could carry off and return home with few or no losses, and the War Raid, which was to avenge the death of a kinsman who lost his or her life in a battle with the enemy.[71]

The three basic principles of Apache tactics were evasion, ambush and attack.[72] Evasion avoided the enemy as much as possible until there was an opportunity to attack or escape. To evade, Apache warriors operated in small groups, but always keeping in communication. This was accomplished by the use of signals, usually mirror flashes or smoke from fires. General Philip Sheridan summed up evasion saying, "Their tactics being to attack and plunder some given point, then to scatter like quails and meet again at some other distant point previously understood, for plunder and again scatter; therefore, it is exceedingly difficult for our troops to over taken and punish them."[73]

Apaches used elements of native spirituality to evade the enemy. Lozen, Victorio's sister, was noted for her ability to locate the enemy. James

Kaywaykla was with Victorio as a young man and said, "Many times I have seen her, stand with her hands outstretched, she would slowly turn as she sang a prayer." Using this power, Lozen was able to find the approaching military and scouts and predict their movements. Her power allowed Victorio to avoid the army or to plan an ambush.[74]

Setting the ambush was key to Apache victory. Apaches watched the advancing troops, looking for any weakness in their daily routine or line of march. Then, using knowledge of the terrain, concealment and discipline, the Apaches would allow the military to walk or be decoyed into a trap.

The first phase of the attack was to destroy the enemy's ability to respond in the first volley. The Apaches targeted the cavalry's horses and the mules loaded with supplies. With the first phase completed, the Apaches would then pin down the troops, picking them off one by one.

Sylvester Grover, a cavalry veteran, recalled in 1925 an Apache ambush in 1885 in New Mexico. "I was shot and lying two and a half hours under a burning sun without water, I felt that my last moments were coming." Then, suddenly, the Apaches were gone just as a relief column arrived.[75]

Once the attack was broken off, the Apaches would again separate into small groups. Each member of the warrior band knew the objectives, the location of the assembly point and the location of where weapons and supplies were hidden.[76]

Many Apaches used traditional weapons, such as the bow and arrow, lance, sling and club. However, once the repeating rifle became common, the Apaches were able to arm themselves with rapid-fire weapons.[77] In 1883, General Crook's troops found the Apaches to be armed with both Winchester and Springfield breechloaders, as well as revolvers.[78] The Apaches procured their weapons from many sources. Some were gained in raids and others from trading with gunrunners in the United States and Mexico, and some were issued on the reservations by the Indian Bureau to be used for hunting. Colonel Benjamin H. Grierson of the Tenth Cavalry criticized the Department of the Interior, saying that the Mescalero Agency was "virtually a supply camp for Victorio's Band."[79]

Apache tactics allowed small bands of Apache warriors to outfight and outmaneuver large units of the United States military. Very early on in the Apache Wars, the military became convinced that the Apaches were never going to be conquered by United States troops or by civilian volunteers or any combination of the two. Success would depend on adopting Apache tactics and the enlistment of Indians to serve as scouts.[80]

Chapter 6

NAVAJO SCOUTS TAKE THE FIELD

I n the summer of 1873, Major William Redwood Price took five companies of the Eighth Cavalry (five hundred men) and twenty-five Navajo scouts to Fort Stanton, arriving there on August 28. Before arriving at Stanton, Price's troops had recovered stolen livestock in the area near Fort Bayard from several groups of Ojo Caliente (Warm Springs) Apaches.[81] Major Price's mission at Fort Stanton was also to recover livestock taken from off-reservation ranchers by the Mescalero Apaches. During this campaign, several small battles were fought with Apache bands. Navajo scout Vincintie Begay recalled Price's campaign, in which he served as first sergeant of scouts:

> *There was a small skirmish while we were there. The white captain, name not known to me, sent Jose Chavez, Mariana Begay, and Guytanio on some scout duty as they saw a* [Apache] *man riding up a draw, we went to the top of the hill and the Apaches opened fire on us and Mariana Begay got off his horse and the Apaches shot and killed it, and they* [Apaches] *wounded my horse in the shoulder, we were able to capture some horses and took them back to camp and the captain sent us back with the horses where we found them and we turned them loose there with the exception of the horse to replace the one killed. We went south from there and we scouted all summer and went back to Fort Wingate.*[82]

Price's troops were in the saddle all that summer, moving south into the Guadalupe Mountains and onto the plains of West Texas. Major

Right: Major William Redwood Price, born in Ohio, served in the Civil War and the Indian Wars. *Courtesy of Wikimedia Commons.*

Below: Fort Bayard, New Mexico, 1886. *U.S. Army Signal Corps, courtesy of Place of the Governors Photo Archive, New Mexico History Museum (NMHM/DCS), #001663.*

Price was able to drive hostile bands of Mescaleros into Mexico, but he was not able to keep the Mescaleros on the reservation or recover much stolen livestock.[83]

In 1874, Major Price again led Navajo scouts. On August 28, with three companies of the Eighth Cavalry, two mountain howitzers and a company of Navajo scouts, he left Fort Bascom for Indian Territory. After a stop at Fort Union, the column moved down the Canadian River for a planned meeting with troops of the Sixth Cavalry, but on the way, Price's troops approached a battle in progress. Comanches and Kiowas were attacking an army supply wagon train under the command of Captain Wyllys Lyman. Price's advance guard was confronted by a party of Kiowa warriors. The scouts and troops did not engage the Indians but rather drew into a defensive circle. The Indians also did not attack, instead circling the cavalry and scouts for two hours and then withdrawing.[84] After the Kiowas withdrew, the troops continued their march. Civilian army scout Thompson McFadden noted this action in his diary:

> *That on a nice bright morning, we moved down the river one and one-half miles where there was good grass and go into camp. We now proceed to dry our water soaked blankets and clean up our equipment. A shot from our vidette* [mounted sentry] *on post about one-half mile out brings a call, "To horse, to horse." We hastily saddle up and gallop out to ascertain the cause of the alarm. We saw Indians, but soon recognized white men, too. The party was the advance guard of Major Price's command, the Eighth Cavalry for whom we had been looking so long in vain. The Indians were Navajo Scouts who had accompanied him from New Mexico. The mystery of the Indians abandoning the siege of our train, was now explained. The Indians had discovered the approach of Price who was accidentally coming directly toward the place where the train was corralled. I was detailed with three of the scouts to accompany the supply train with the wounded men to Camp Supply eighty-eight miles away.*[85]

This expedition into Indian Territory, to take part in the Red River War, showed the sometimes bitter rivalry between the army and the Indian Bureau. Agent to the Navajos W.F.M. Arny complained bitterly that Major Price had recruited Navajo scouts and taken them to the Colorado plains without his permission, but the Navajos' devotion to duty won them many friends in the military.[86]

Indian agent W.F.M. Arny, 1875. *Courtesy of Place of the Governors Photo Archive, New Mexico History Museum (NMHM/DCS), #008789.*

Navajo Scouts During the Apache Wars

The year 1875 was a peaceful one, and no Navajos were recruited as scouts; however, a government policy known as the "Concentration of Indian Tribes" would end any hope of peace in the Southwest.

The concentration policy was a response to the increase of the white population on the frontier and the conflict between the two peoples. It was first begun under the Lincoln administration; Commissioner of Indian Affairs William P. Dole noted that "the plan of concentration of Indians and confining them to reservations may now be regarded as the fixed policy of the government."[87] For white reformers, this policy seemed to be the most beneficial for both the Indian and the American populations. Settlers would gain lands opened to them by Indian removal. Indians would gain by the establishment of a home safe from the pressures of settler encroachment on these lands. They would also benefit from annuities of tools and goods. Once concentrated on reservations, the Indians would be exposed to the full blessings of the American culture, religion and English language. The rub, as historian Robert Utley stated, was that "before this blessing could be bestowed, however, the Indians had to be concentrated."[88]

The attempt by the Indian Bureau to carry out this policy and concentrate Apaches on a single reservation at San Carlos, Arizona, served as the major cause of the Apache Wars during the late 1870s and early 1880s. This move broke the agreements negotiated by various Apache bands and Vincent Colyer for the United States during the early 1870s.[89]

The Ojo Caliente Apaches openly resisted this policy. The Ojo Calientes firmly believed that the area located between the Black Range of the Mimbres Mountains and the San Mateo Mountains had been granted to them by the "Holy People" to inhabit and care for forever. In 1871, the United States government moved these people to a reservation at the foot of the Tularosa Mountains some fifty miles west of Ojo Caliente. This move proved to be a failure because the growing season was too short to sustain farming.

As discussed earlier, in the summer of 1872, General Oliver O. Howard, special Indian commissioner, visited the Southwest to explain the Grant administration's peace policy to all Indian nations. During this tour, Howard met Victorio and other Ojo Caliente leaders. Howard told Victorio's people that they would be able to return to Ojo Caliente if Chiricahua chief Cochise was willing to move the Chiricahuas there. Cochise later refused, and his people were placed on a reservation in southeastern Arizona. The government, not knowing what to do with the Ojo Calientes, established a reservation for them in their homeland.[90]

Navajo Scouts During the Apache Wars

In the winter and spring of 1875–76, the Ninth Cavalry moved from West Texas to New Mexico[91] in response to unrest throughout Apacheria produced by the government's continued concentration of Apache groups on reservations in Arizona and citizen pressure to open more Apache lands to settlement. This move was to deal with Apache bands that were leaving the reservation or refusing to be placed on reservations and raiding settlements in Arizona and New Mexico. The Ninth Cavalry was posted at Forts Bayard, McRae, Wingate and Union, with one company at Garland in Colorado. The Ninth was spread thin over the Southwest and would need the support of Indian scouts and civilian volunteers. To make matters worse for the Buffalo Soldiers in New Mexico, the Apaches were heavily armed with late-model weapons, including Springfield Carbines and Smith & Wesson revolvers.[92] As a part of this buildup, in May 1876 Major Henry H. Wright enlisted twenty-five Navajo scouts at Fort Wingate to serve with the Ninth Cavalry.[93]

By the new year of 1877, Major Wright and the Navajo scouts had been posted at Fort Bayard in southern New Mexico. In late January, word reached the fort that a party of Chiricahua Apaches had skirmished with

Buffalo Soldiers of the Ninth Cavalry at Fort Wingate. *Phelps, courtesy of Place of the Governors Photo Archive, New Mexico History Museum (NMHM/DCS), #098372.*

elements of the Sixth Cavalry in Arizona and was thought to be moving into New Mexico. Major Wright, along with six troopers of Company C and three Navajo scouts, were sent out to locate the Chiricahua camp. On January 24, the Navajo scouts picked up the trail in the Florida Mountains and located the Apache camp with fifty warriors. Wright did not attack but rather entered the camp peacefully and began to talk to the Apaches. The talks had lasted about half an hour when Wright noticed that he was being surrounded. He broke off the talks and ordered his men to push through the warriors. After a short exchange of rifle and pistol fire, the fighting turned hand-to-hand with the Apaches, Navajo scouts and Buffalo Soldiers using their weapons as clubs. Singlehandedly, Corporal Clifton Greaves managed to open a gap through the Apaches, which allowed his comrades to escape. Once the soldiers broke free, the Apaches, who had lost five warriors, abandoned their camp, leaving the cavalry in possession of five horses and various supplies. Remarkably, the troopers and scouts had no serious casualties. Corporal Greaves was awarded the Congressional Medal of Honor for his actions, and troopers Richard Epps, Dick Mackadoo, John Adams and Navajo scout Jose Chavez were all commended for bravery in action.[94]

Fort Wingate, New Mexico, 1873. *T. O'Sullivan, courtesy of National Archives and Records, Washington, D.C., #106-WB-325.*

Navajo Scouts During the Apache Wars

Captain Henry H. Wright and Navajos (possibly scouts) at Fort Defiance, 1872–78. *Henry T. Hiester, courtesy of Place of the Governors Photo Archive, New Mexico History Museum (NMHM/DCS), #038035.*

The Ojo Caliente people were happy to be home, and all went well until the spring of 1877, when the United States government, in a plan to save money and administrative costs, moved all Apaches, including those in New Mexico, to a large reservation at San Carlos, Arizona. On April 30, 1877, the Buffalo Soldiers escorted 435 Ojo Caliente Apaches away from their homes to the San Carlos Reservation. The Ojo Caliente people were forced to leave with their crops unharvested and make the trek to Arizona, where they were obligated to share the same location with other groups of Apaches, some of whom were their traditional rivals. Geronimo and other troublemakers were transported in a wagon as chained prisoners.[95]

Ojo Caliente leader Victorio had been in Arizona for only a few months when he led three hundred Ojo Caliente Apache men, women and children out of San Carlos into the nearby Natanes Mountains. In need of horses and supplies, the Apaches began raiding ranches and mining camps, killing twelve settlers and capturing more than one hundred head of livestock. A combined force of army patrols and Apache police attempted to return Victorio and his people to San Carlos, but they were able to escape into New Mexico. There, they fought several battles with elements of the Ninth Cavalry supported by Navajo scouts.[96]

Navajo scout Nargito remembered some aspects of the scouts' effort to return Victorio to San Carlos:

> *We enlisted at Fort Wingate and worked down to Fort Bayard and scouted from there for a long time and* [then] *we were over to Ojo Caliente two times and had some brushes with Apaches. We* [also] *went over once to near San Carlos where there were some soldiers and they took charge of some Apache captives* [we had]. *We went back to* [Fort Bayard] *and then to the Mescalero Apache Reservation and scouted there for a while, then back to Fort Wingate and were discharged.*[97]

Navajo scout Hosteen Cly (aka Barbon Segundo) recalled that seven Navajo scouts and troops went after the Apaches from Fort Bayard, following them into the Magdalena Mountains. On this trip, Navajo scouts captured three Apache men and three women. The men were able to escape, but the women were killed. A baby with one of the women was wounded in the heel. The troops and scouts then returned to Fort Bayard. After two months patrolling from Bayard, they went to Ojo Caliente and escorted a group of Apaches to San Carlos, where they were turned over to the soldiers. From San Carlos, the scouts returned to Fort Wingate and were discharged.[98]

Since leaving San Carlos, the Ojo Caliente people were relentlessly pursued by Buffalo Soldiers, supported by Apache police and Navajo scouts. Victorio soon realized that returning to Ojo Caliente was no longer possible, as the army had occupied their former agency. Faced with this fact, Victorio planned escape into old Mexico but soon found that the army had cut off all the trails leading south.[99]

Having faith in the ability of his sister, Lozen, a war leader and medicine woman gifted with the power to locate and avoid enemy patrols, Victorio was able to lead his people into the safety of the lava beds south of Fort Wingate. Although safe in the malpais, the Apaches were short of food and totally without clothing and weapons. Their horse herd was depleted and worn out, and there was no chance to capture more due to the unrelenting cavalry patrols. Consulting with other leaders Loco, Chivo and Lozen, Victorio sent word to the officers at Fort Wingate that he would surrender if his people were not forced to return to San Carlos.[100] Earlier, Colonel Edward Hatch, expecting a surrender offer, had sent orders that any Apache willing to come to Fort Wingate was to be fed and cared for.[101]

On September 29, Thomas Keam left Fort Wingate with two Ojo Caliente Apaches and five Navajo scouts to meet with Victorio. Keam had been hired by the army as an interpreter and had recently been appointed as temporary superintendent for the Apaches who had surrendered at Fort Wingate.[102]

Thomas Varker Keam had served with the California Volunteers during the Civil War and was stationed at Fort Sumner during the Navajo internment. While there, he developed a working knowledge of both the Mescalero Apache and Navajo languages. In addition, his service with the New Mexico Volunteers had also allowed him to become proficient in Spanish. In 1869, he was mustered out of the army and was hired as an interpreter at Fort Defiance, Arizona, the Navajo Agency, and soon after he married Asdzaan Liba, a Navajo woman. Keam became popular with the Navajos and the army, and following the death of Agent James H. Miller in 1872, he was appointed special agent to the Navajos.[103] Over time, Keam developed personal friendships with several Navajo leaders, including Manuelito and Mariano. In 1872, Keam along with Manuelito and General Howard established the Navajo cavalry.[104]

Notwithstanding the support of the Navajos and the army, Keam was not selected as permanent agent. The Presbyterian Board of Foreign Mission, which had the power to recommend Indian Bureau employees, objected to Keam because of his marriage to a Navajo woman. Without this endorsement, Keam could not be hired as agent. The man chosen as agent, W.F.M. Arny, expelled Keam and several other "Squaw Men" from the Navajo Reservation, declaring that "[a]ny white man who married an Indian was a lost soul and unfit to remain in the presence of decent white men."[105]

Keam, however, was the best man to carry out the task of meeting with Victorio. On October 3, Keam met with the Apaches near their camp at

Ojo del Gallo. At this meeting, Keam told the Apaches that his purpose was to take them to Fort Wingate. Several of the Apache leaders said that not all the people wished to surrender. Keam asked them to separate those who wished to go to Wingate and those who wanted to stay in the mountains. However, Keam said, he would be responsible only for those who went to Fort Wingate. Those who remained, Keam warned, would have troops sent after them. At that point, many Apaches agreed to go to Fort Wingate with Keam and the Navajo scouts. Rations were then issued to the 179 Apaches with Victorio.

On the trail to Fort Wingate, Keam talked to Apache leaders, telling them that the Americans were not going anywhere and that the only way they could keep their families was to cooperate with the Americans. Keam used the Navajos as an example, pointing out their improved conditions since Fort Sumner, and noted that cooperation could also benefit the Apaches. The Apache leaders told Keam that they would cooperate if the army would let them return to Ojo Caliente.[106]

Not all the Apaches had come in with Victorio. Navajo leader Mariano, who had in-laws among the Apaches, and scout John Navajo led separate expeditions to persuade small groups of Apaches to come to Fort Wingate for rations and protection.[107]

By October 11, post commander Captain Jewett had reported that 233 Apaches had surrendered at Fort Wingate; however, Victorio's uncle Nana and a small group of Apaches did not come in and remained in the mountains.

Thomas Keam remained in charge of the Apaches at Fort Wingate, escorting them on hunts and giving them permission to pick piñon nuts in the Zuni Mountains. Then, in late fall, Colonel Edward Hatch ordered that the Apaches return to Ojo Caliente under the supervision of Keam.

By the spring, the Apaches were planting crops and settling into a peaceful life. Keam informed Colonel Hatch that the Apaches were almost daily coming to him and asking that their relatives at San Carlos be returned to them at Ojo Caliente. Keam wrote to Hatch that he thought it would be an act of humanity that their families be brought from San Carlos, and Hatch agreed. Keam also requested from Captain A.E. Hooker of the Ninth Cavalry that farming tools be provided and noted that the Apaches needed the help of their families to care for crops during the growing season. Keam also told Hooker that he needed to return to his trading post near Fort Defiance, and by mid-March, his duties with the Apaches were finished.[108]

Chapter 7

THE VICTORIO WAR

In August 1878, the United States government made the decision to return the Ojo Caliente people to San Carlos. The determination to again move the Apaches was made after discussion between the army, the Indian Bureau and the Apaches themselves. The Indian Bureau initially favored moving the band to the San Carlos Reservation or to Indian Territory, while the army suggested the Mescalero Reservation in southern New Mexico, even though Victorio wanted only to stay at Ojo Caliente. After further discussions, the Indian Bureau agreed to Mescalero, but the army changed its mind and thought that San Carlos would be better. In June 1879, Victorio agreed and moved to the Mescalero Reservation.[109]

When the decision was made to send the Ojo Caliente Apaches to San Carlos, Captain Frank Bennett of the Ninth Cavalry was ordered to escort them. He left Fort Wingate with two companies of cavalry and one company of Navajo scouts. The escort force arrived at Mescalero on October 8 to begin the removal. Bennett met with the Ojo Caliente Apaches to persuade them to go peacefully to San Carlos. Because Victorio, Loco and other leaders were at Fort Wingate, the Apaches refused to take any action until their leaders returned. On October 12, Victorio and the other leaders returned, and the talks resumed. Bennett reported that Victorio said that his people did not want to leave their present home, but they would go if necessary. However, they would not go to San Carlos. They claimed that the Apaches there were unfriendly, having taken some of the Ojo Calientes' livestock and weapons. Also, Victorio said the water was bad and his people got sick from

Navajo Scouts During the Apache Wars

Victorio, leader of the Ojo Caliente Apaches. *Courtesy of National Anthropological Archives, Washington, D.C., #02277400.*

it. On October 14, Victorio, because he saw no hope to change this decision, agreed to go, but the next night he and eighty of his warriors escaped into the mountains.

Bennett sent Lieutenant Henry H. Wright and Navajo scouts, who had much experience in tracking Apaches, to find the escapees, but they were unable to locate the fleeing Apaches due to heavy rains that washed out their trail. Captain Bennett put the remaining Apaches under guard, which set off a panic and more people fled. Again, Wright's Navajo scouts were sent out, but they were able only to locate a woman and three children. Finally, on October 25, Bennett began the march to San Carlos with six wagons, a small herd of cattle and horses belonging to the Apaches and the remaining 173 Apaches, mostly women and children, under the leadership of headman Loco. The weather did not ease the journey for the military or the Apaches. It rained and snowed continuously, causing the roads to become a mud-bog and impassible to the wagons. Captain Bennett sent a courier to request pack mules to replace the now useless wagons. On November 15, a courier brought word that allowed Bennett to purchase mules and other supplies.

Captain Bennett and Manuelito in the 1880s. *Henry T. Hiester, courtesy of Place of the Governors Photo Archive, New Mexico History Museum (NMHM/DCS), #038029.*

But on the same day, Dan Ming, the chief of the Apache Indian police, arrived with thirty-eight Apache Indian police officers to take charge of the prisoners of war. The Apaches were now under the control of the Indian Bureau. The Ojo Caliente Apaches reached San Carlos on November 25, all having survived the march. On the first day of December, Captain Bennett and his Navajo scouts and Buffalo Solders returned to Fort Wingate after a 719-mile trek.[110]

Navajo Scouts During the Apache Wars

Buffalo Soldiers in the winter. *Courtesy of Wikimedia Commons.*

In the months after Victorio and his followers fled into the mountains, small war bands began raiding isolated ranches and settlements in western and southern New Mexico. To the surprise of everyone, Victorio and his followers entered Ojo Caliente in February 1879 and informed Lieutenant Charles W. Merritt that he would surrender if he and his people could stay at Ojo Caliente. Merritt contacted General Hatch, who informed the War Department. Nothing happened until April, when Victorio was told that he must go to the Mescalero Agency. Victorio and his followers again went into the mountains, but in June, the whole band arrived at Mescalero. The agent there, S.A. Russell, told Victorio that if his people agreed to settle down, farm and live in peace, their families could be returned from San Carlos. Victorio agreed to these conditions.

The plan to settle the Ojo Caliente Apaches at Mescalero ignited a fury among the settlers and the New Mexico press. A grand jury met in Silver City and issued an indictment against Victorio and his followers for murder and rustling. When word of the indictment reached Victorio, he angrily told agent Russell that he was a liar. Russell responded that he was going to issue more ration tickets to Victorio and his band. Victorio told the agent that there were other things besides rations and that he was leaving Mescalero in three days. He then tore the rations tickets to shreds and threw them in Russell's face. After Victorio's angry departure, Russell sent for help from Fort Stanton. In record time, a cavalry force arrived, but Victorio and the Ojo Calientes were gone, along with a large number of Mescaleros. Victorio now had a force of 150 fighting men.[111]

Victorio had had enough. It was now a war of survival. His forces struck first, raiding a horse camp under the command of Lieutenant Ambrose Hooker, killing five Buffalo Soldiers and three civilian herders. At the same time, another force of Ojo Caliente Apaches hit the H.D. McEver Ranch, fifteen miles south of Hillsboro, New Mexico, killing ten civilians and taking all the livestock and supplies.[112]

Shortly after Victorio's raid on September 4, 1879, at the McEver Ranch, Lieutenant Colonel Dudley, with a force of the Ninth Cavalry and Navajo Indian scouts, began a pursuit of Victorio's Apaches.[113] Since September 5, Lieutenant Henry Wright with a party of Buffalo Soldiers and Navajo Indian scouts had searched for Apaches in the Socorro Mountains. However, finding none, he received orders to join a force of the Ninth Cavalry and three Navajo scouts led by Captain Byron Dawson and Lieutenant Matthias Day at the McEver Ranch.[114] At the ranch, Dawson's Navajo scouts quickly located the Apaches' trail. The trail was now two days old, but the Apaches were slowed by the number of women and children in their party and the herd of horses they had gained from the raid on Lieutenant Ambrose Hooker's horse herd on September 4.[115]

On September 18, 1879, as the troops entered a side canyon near where it joins Las Animas Creek, they were fired on by an Apache woman and two men. At this point, the troops advanced into the canyon. Ignoring the warning of the Navajo scouts not to enter the canyon, the cavalry chased the three Apaches across an open meadow and into the canyon. The entrance was very narrow, about thirty yards wide, and had rock spires on each side.[116] Once the troops had entered the canyon, a Navajo scout began to climb the rock wall of the canyon for a better look. He was killed by a single shot.[117] Then all the Apaches opened fire. The first volleys killed most of the horses and left Dawson's men on foot and pinned down. Dawson determined that retreat was impossible and established a defensive perimeter.

Captain Charles Beyer, whose troops had not entered the canyon, heard the gunfire and, with his troops and civilian volunteers from the town of Hillsboro, prepared to advance. Beyer, leaving a small detachment outside the canyon as a rear guard under Lieutenant Robert Emmet, rode to the sound of gunfire to support Dawson.[118] Victorio's warriors held their fire until Beyer's troops were within range and then renewed the fight.[119] Beyer's arrival may have saved Dawson's detachment from being overrun, as the cavalry now outnumbered the Apaches. However, they found themselves unable to dislodge the Apaches from their positions on the canyon rim.[120] Now Victorio had two elements of the Ninth pinned downed, separated and dismounted.[121]

Navajo Scouts During the Apache Wars

The battle lasted all day, with Beyer's troops unable to flank the Apaches and unite with Dawson. At dusk, the troops withdrew under the covering fire of the rear guard, leaving their equipment and the few horses still alive.

The battle at Las Animas was a victory for the Apaches, having forced the retreat of a superior force, inflicting casualties and capturing equipment. The United States lost eight troopers, two civilians and two Navajo scouts. In addition, eighty-five horses were killed or captured. The military found no evidence of any Apache casualties.[122]

Navajo scout Nostohe recalled years later that "we were attacked by the Apache and had to fight them, two of our Navajo Scouts were killed."[123]

Three soldiers—Lieutenant Robert Temple Emmet, Lieutenant Mathias Day and Sergeant John Denny—each received the Congressional Medal of Honor for acts of bravery during the battle. Navajo scout Hostensorze (Hosteen Tsosie) was cited for bravery by the army, as were Lieutenant Wright, Mr. Foster, Sergeant Penn, Sergeant Lyman, Sergeant Boyne and Privates Malry and Ridgely.[124]

For the next two years, fighting raged between the United States Army and Victorio's followers. James Kaywaykla was a youth at the time of the Victorio War and recalled, "Until I was ten years old, I did not know that people died except by violence."[125]

In order to deal with Apache raids against mining camps and ranches, the military increased its forces in West Texas, New Mexico and Arizona. The Ninth Cavalry in New Mexico was reinforced by the Sixth Cavalry from Arizona. Five companies of the Thirteenth Infantry were sent to Fort Wingate, and the Tenth Cavalry was sent from Texas to southern Arizona and New Mexico. Also, a unit of the Texas Rangers joined the hunt for Victorio.[126] The number of Indian scouts was increased, and scouts were enlisted from several groups of Apaches: Lipan, White Mountain and San Carlos. In addition to Navajos, scouts from the New Mexico Pueblos, Papago (Tohno O'odham), Walapais and other tribes were enlisted.[127]

The use of so many different tribes as scouts makes it difficult to know what scout companies took part in an action. Military written reports of the time mention the officer in charge of the unit, the location of the action and the result of the action. In many cases, scouts are listed only as "Indian Scouts," without tribal identification. Because so many scout companies were in the field, it is difficult to determine what particular group of scouts stayed with a particular officer, unless named in the action report.[128]

After two victories over the Mexican army in Mexico, Victorio returned to United States territory and began a campaign of raiding along the border.

Victorio's success resulted in groups of Mescalero and Lipan Apaches, Comanches and even some Navajos, all unhappy with reservation life, joining with Victorio's dissidents.[129]

In response to Victorio's growing strength, Hatch took personal command of a force composed of five troops of the Tenth Cavalry, a detachment of the Ninth Cavalry, one company of the Fifteenth Infantry and a company of Navajo scouts from Fort Bayard.[130] From Arizona, a troop of the Sixth Cavalry, with three Apache scout companies, all moved into place to block any escape route Victorio might use, all in an attempt to defeat the Ojo Caliente Apaches once and for all.[131]

Western newspapers reported that William T. Sherman had given Hatch carte blanche to feed and arm all Navajos and others who may desire to join the troops in the campaign against Victorio. Sherman warned, however, that no one may act independently of United States forces. In response, Chief Mariano of the Navajos offered himself and one hundred warriors to go on the warpath against Victorio. Mariano asked only that he be given rations and arms.[132]

Hatch learned that Victorio's band was safely camped in the Hembrillo Canyon and planned to push them out of their stronghold. But the plan went wrong when Captain Henry Carroll failed to link up with Major Morrow's troops, who were delayed because they drank contaminated water from a spring and both horses and men became ill. Carroll's troops, without scouts, walked into an ambush. Pinned down for almost a day, they

Sixth Cavalry Band at Fort Wingate, 1880s. *John Landerdale, 1889, courtesy of Beinecke Library Yale University, #3724294.*

General William T. Sherman. *Courtesy of Wikimedia Commons.*

were finally rescued by Captain McLellan's San Carols Apache scouts, led by Lieutenant Gatewood.[133]

After the army's failure to defeat the Ojo Calientes at the Battle of Hembrillo Canyon, where bad water and bad luck led to near disaster,[134] Hatch continued a move to disarm the Mescalero Reservation. On April 16, 1880, Hatch arrived at the Mescalero Reservation with a large force of troops, including Apache and Navajo scouts, and told the agent that there was clear evidence that Victorio was being supplied with arms and supplies coming from Mescalero. The agent, S.A. Russell, protested that the Mescaleros were peaceful and that the military had no authority on the reservation.[135] Hatch told Russell that he planned to disarm all Mescaleros. Agent Russell had requested the Mescaleros come to the agency on April 17 to draw rations, and about 320, mostly women and children, were present. When the army began to search for weapons and seize horses, gunshots were heard and a general melee broke out. When it was all over, forty Mescaleros had been killed. While the violent action had taken only a few weapons and horses, it had increased the support for Victorio.[136]

Colonel Hatch returned to Santa Fe to report his "success" at disarming the Mescaleros. The Tenth Cavalry returned to Texas, and the Sixth Cavalry and the Apache scouts returned to Arizona. The Ninth Cavalry, with Navajo scouts, began a search in the Black Range for the hostile Apaches.

Victorio was not idle during the Hatch campaign. In April, his forces struck Alma, New Mexico, killing forty-one settlers in that region. Also in April, bands of Victorio's followers attacked the troops of Company K of the Ninth Cavalry at Fort Tularosa. In early May, Victorio himself led an attack on the San Carlos Reservation to free the Ojo Caliente families held

A line of Apaches waiting for rations at San Carlos. *Courtesy of Beinecke Library Yale University, WA 142 #137470.*

there and to capture livestock and supplies. This raid was also directed at the families of White Mountain Apaches serving with the military, and several were killed in this raid.

It was clear to Colonel Hatch that the fight at Hembrillo Canyon accomplished little to discourage Victorio and that the disarmament of the Mescalero Agency had done more harm than good. Faced with the territorial press calling for the army to do something, Hatch decided to send Apaches against Apaches and allowed his civilian chief of scouts, Henry K. Parker, to take a force of fifty Apache scouts to look for Victorio's band.

Parker's scouts located Victorio's camp after dark on May 23, 1880, and attacked at dawn the next day. The first volley took the camp by surprise, and many Apaches fell before they could respond. The remainder recovered quickly and dug rifle pits and other makeshift defenses. The battle lasted most of the day until Parker's force had to break off the engagement due to lack of ammunition.

Given a chance to escape, Apache survivors retreated into Mexico. Victorio had lost thirty of his people, including several women who had fought alongside the warriors. Victorio himself was wounded. In Mexico, the band was able to regroup, and in a few months, small groups began to raid into Arizona and New Mexico. But Victorio and other hostile Apaches were beginning to lose spirit. Historian Paul Hutton called the Battle of Palomas River the turning point of the Victorio War.[137]

The U.S. military began to build its forces for a final blow against Victorio. Colonel George P. Buell organized a mixed force of cavalry, infantry and Indian scouts to enter Mexico. The Mexican government had agreed to allow the U.S. military to enter its territory when in pursuit of Apaches.

In Mexico, Colonel Joaquin Terrazas, with 350 Mexican militiamen and Tarahumara Indian scouts, closed in on Victorio's exhausted band. Terrazas asked that American troops leave Mexico, as he wished to have the sole honor of defeating Victorio.

In the Mexican state of Chihuahua at Tres Castillos, in October, the Mexican militia caught up with Victorio. In a two-day battle, Victorio was killed and many of his people captured and sold into slavery by the Mexicans. Only a few escaped or were not present at Tres Castillos. However, two of the survivors who were with Victorio's uncle Nana and his sister, Lozen, along with others, would carry on the resistance.[138]

Chapter 8

NANA'S RAID

Nana, a man in his seventies, was able to regroup the remains of Victorio's band and lead them to the safety of the Florida Mountains in New Mexico. There, he was joined by Lozen, who left the Mescalero Agency when she heard of the defeat at Tres Castillos and was able to find Nana and the others in the mountains.[139] From their base in the mountains, Nana's warriors began a campaign to avenge Victorio, based on a series of raids carried out by small bands of warriors designed to inflict as many casualties as possible on their enemies.[140]

During the summer of 1881, Nana, with a force of no more than forty warriors, led a two-month-long series of raids, covering one thousand miles that resulted in the death of thirty civilians and five soldiers and the capture of two hundred head of livestock.[141]

Navajo scouts took part in several of the eight skirmishes in which the army engaged Nana's raiding parties. One of the more notable of Navajo scouts' action concerns the raid on Rancho Cebolla, located south of the present location of Grants, New Mexico.

On the morning of August 8, 1881, a party of Apaches accompanied by a group of Navajos arrived at the ranch of Domingo and Placida Gallegos and their infant daughter, Trinidad. Also present that morning was Jose Maria Vargas, Domingo's business partner. Domingo knew the Navajos, for he had at times traded with them in the past. Therefore, he was not suspicious when he was asked to show off his shooting skills. Domingo obliged, shooting at targets until his gun was empty. He was then shot down

Apache leader Nana. *Ben Wittick, 1880s, courtesy of Place of the Governors Photo Archive, New Mexico History Museum (NMHM/DCS), #016321.*

by one of the Apaches. Jose Maria Vargas ran to Domingo's aide, but he too was murdered. The Indians then forced Placida and her baby to mount a horse and leave with them.[142]

On August 11, while in pursuit of Apache raiders, troops of the Ninth Cavalry under Lieutenant Guilfoye and Lieutenant Henry H. Wright, with

Navajo Scouts During the Apache Wars

Above: A New Mexican family, 1880s. *James E. Taylor, courtesy of National Anthropological Archives, Washington, D.C., #NAA INV 01600111.*

Right: Settler killed by Apaches south of Fort Wingate. *Ben Wittick, courtesy of Place of the Governors Photo Archive, New Mexico History Museum (NMHM/DCS), #055582.*

Navajo scouts, reached Rancho Cebolla and found the bodies of Domingo and Jose Maria. Wright sent a courier to the telegraph at McCarty's to inform the commander at Fort Wingate of the events at Rancho Cebolla. Wright and his scouts followed the trail of Nana's raiders, but due to heavy rains, they were not able to continue the chase. Wright reported later that having heard no more news of the raiders, and given that his scouts' enlistments were up, he returned to Fort Wingate.[143]

One day later, on August 12, one wing of Nana's band fought an engagement with Captain Charles Parker's Apache scouts. The Apaches broke off the fight and headed southeast toward Sierra Ladron through what is now the Alamo Navajo reservation.[144] On August 16, Lieutenant George Burnett's troops followed the hostiles into the Cuchillo Negro Mountain in the Black Range. On April 18, Nana's forces bypassed Burnett advance guard but were pushed into Second Lieutenant Charles William Taylor's company of Navajo scouts out of Ojo Caliente. A short skirmish followed in which several of the scouts' horses were killed. After the fight, Taylor's scouts reported to him that Placida Gallegos, the woman captured at Rancho Cebolla, was with this band.[145] The Navajo scouts pursued the Apaches but were unable to make contact.

The Apaches now moved into the Black Range west of Ojo Caliente, leaving a trail of burned-out ranches and murdered settlers in their wake. The people in the town of Hillsboro, alarmed by the violence of the raid, formed a posse of local volunteers determined to clear the area of Apaches. The posse, led by George Daly, manager of local mines, reach the town of Lake Valley on August 18 and found another group of volunteers ready to join them.

Camped near Lake Valley were two companies of the Ninth Cavalry, commanded by Second Lieutenant George Washington Smith. The civilian volunteers were ready to move forward, but Lieutenant Smith did not want to advance without Taylor's scouts. Daly and his volunteers accused the troops of being lazy and cowardly and left in search of the Apaches. Smith, not wanting to leave the volunteers on their own, joined them. On August 19, at 10:00 a.m., in Dry Gavilan Canyon, they walked into an Apache ambush in which both Smith and Daly were killed in the first volley. If not for the courage under fire of Sergeant Brent Wood, the entire command would have been destroyed. In addition to the deaths of several civilians and soldiers, thirty horses and pack mules loaded with one thousand rounds of ammunition fell into Nana's hands.

A Navajo scout who served with Lieutenant Guilfoye. *Ben Wittick, courtesy of Place of the Governors Photo Archive, New Mexico History Museum (NMHM/DCS), #015936.*

At about four o'clock in the afternoon, Companies B and H of the Ninth Cavalry and Lieutenant Taylor's Navajo scouts entered Gavilan Canyon to find the troops and civilians behind makeshift barricades and the bodies of the dead lying where they fell. The Apaches had withdrawn, taking their spoils with them. No pursuit of the Apaches was undertaken due to the lateness of the day.

The victory at Gavilan Canyon allowed Nana and his followers to escape into the Florida Mountains, and then on August 23, they fled into Mexico, taking young Placida Gallegos with them. Her infant daughter, Trinidad, had been left with a Navajo family somewhere south of Grants. After months in the mountains of Mexico, Placida was able to escape and make her way back to Cubero, New Mexico. Upon returning home, she had a daughter fathered by one of her Apache captors who she named Trinidad in memory of the lost Trinidad.[146]

Chapter 9

THE GERONIMO WAR

After Nana's escape to Mexico, the leadership of the Apache resisters was divided among many band leaders, such as Juh, Loco, Ulzana and the aging Nana. But over time, one name stood out, at least in the territorial press, as the leader of the Apache resisters: Geronimo. He was born in about 1829, the grandson of Maco, a Mogollon Apache leader, but his own father married in the Mimbreno (Ojo Caliente) tribe; thus, by Apache custom, he was a Mimbreno himself.[147] His Apache name was Go-ya-thle (He Yawns).

In 1858, Geronimo's wife and mother were killed by Mexican soldiers, leaving Geronimo with a strong desire for revenge against the Mexicans and, later, the Americans. In the view of the Apaches, they seemed to be allied with Mexico against them.

For many years, Geronimo rode with sundry raiding bands hiding in the Sierra Madre of Mexico or drifting into New Mexico or Arizona, visiting various reservation agencies to resupply and recruit. He was at Ojo Caliente in 1877 when the Ojo Caliente people were moved to San Carlos. Because he had already been labeled a dissident, he was removed to San Carlos in chains. In his autobiography, Geronimo noted, "I was kept a prisoner for four months, during which I was sent to San Carlos."[148] Being held a prisoner and shipped in chains was an affront that Geronimo would never forget.[149] He remained at San Carlos for a while, but in 1878, he fled to Mexico to join Nana and Lozen and the exiled Ojo Caliente people.

In 1881, trouble broke out at Fort Apache. Nakaidoklini, known as the Dreamer, himself an ex-scout, began to prophesy that the Americans

Right: Apache leader Geronimo. *Courtesy of Wikimedia Commons.*

Below: Building at San Carlos Reservation (possibly ration storehouse). *Courtesy of Beinecke Library Yale University, New Haven, Connecticut.*

would soon be carried away and long-dead Apaches would return to an earthly paradise inhabited only by Indian people. The Dreamer's ideas drew Apaches and even some Navajos to his village of Cibicue. Although many Navajos were curious about the movement and were dissatisfied with Agent Galen Eastman, none sought to join the followers of the Dreamer.[150]

The military, alarmed by this new religion, sent troops and Apache scouts led by Colonel Eugene A. Carr to arrest the Dreamer. When the military arrived at Cibicue, Nakaidoklini's followers sought to prevent his arrest and fighting broke out, during which the Dreamer was killed by a soldier. The company of Apache scouts was so upset by this that they mutinied and killed their captain. The mutiny of the scouts at Cibicue led to a mistrust of Apache scouts by the army command that would hamper future campaigns against the hostiles and eventually lead to the removal of many Apache scouts from the Southwest. Accounts of the Cibicue massacre filled newspapers all over the country and led to calls for the removal of all Apaches from Arizona. On September 30, 1881, Geronimo and several other Apache leaders and their followers left the reservation for Mexico.

In April 1882, dissident Apaches led by Geronimo and Juh returned to San Carlos, killed the chief of the Apache police and forced Loco and several of his people to go with him to Mexico. Loco, who by this time wanted to remain at peace, developed a mistrust of Geronimo and felt that he had become untrustworthy and dangerous, thus leading the Apaches to certain destruction. He also blamed Geronimo for the loss of the Ojo Caliente reservation and the tribe's removal to San Carlos.

In fact, Loco had begun talks with the army and the Indian Bureau to have the Ojo Caliente people removed to a safer location away from the main Apache reservation. Loco envisioned a move to the Navajo Nation somewhere near Fort Wingate. To support this idea, he contacted Navajo leader Mariano, whose Apache wife was the aunt of two of Loco's wives. Loco gained a pass to leave the reservation and visit Mariano and found both Mariano and Colonel Luther Bradley, commander of Fort Wingate, in support of the plan. On March 25, 1882, Colonel Bradley wrote a letter to Secretary of the Interior Samuel J. Kirkwood, briefing the secretary on the plan:

> *Only one tribe has disposition favoring a removal, namely those known as the Warm Springs Indians. They are related somewhat to the Chiricahuas, the old band of Victorio, and they have some relative among the Navajo. The later have signified a willingness to have them come to live on their*

Navajo Scouts During the Apache Wars

Left: General Eugene Carr. *Courtesy of Library of Congress.*

Right: Apache leader Loco. *Randell A. Frank, 1880, courtesy of Place of Governors Photo Archive, New Mexico History Museum (NMHM/DCS), #0132197.*

> Reservation in New Mexico. The clandestine occasional returns of small parties of Chiricahuas from Mexico is a disturbing element to them. This would be more difficult if they were with the Navajos, whose territory the Chiricahuas have never lived in and is much removed from here.... The tribe here seem to be quite unanimous in the desire to go to the Navajos.[151]

Special Indian inspector Charles Howard also supported the plan and recommended that removal be under the supervision of Navajo scouts and not soldiers. However, the plan got no further because it was opposed by Arizona district commander Orlando B. Willcox, who felt that the Apaches might advise the Navajos to join the hostiles. The plan was also opposed by Galen Eastman, the unpopular Navajo Indian agent, who sent a five-page report to the commissioner of Indian affairs accusing Colonel Bradley of supporting the plan in order to stir up the Navajos and thus provide the army with a pretext to massacre them.[152] Having failed to find a safe refuge for his people, Loco sent his women and children to Fort

Wingate to be under the protection of the military and then joined Geronimo and followed him to Mexico.[153]

By 1883, Geronimo and his followers had become a menace to both the United States and Mexico. Brevet Major General Willcox, commander of the Arizona district, was replaced by General George Crook, whose orders were to end the Apache dissidents' resistance. General Crook supported the idea that the only way to defeat the Apache insurgency was to use large numbers of Indian scouts, who knew the country and the tactics of the dissidents. Crook preferred to use Apaches against Apaches; however, he also sought the aid of other tribes, most notably the Navajos. In 1885, Crook authorized the recruitment of one hundred Navajo scouts.[154]

General Crook. *Courtesy of Wikimedia Commons.*

General Crook's strategy was to establish a loose line of small military outposts along the Mexican border. He then planned to have a force of Apache scouts move in small groups to search and destroy any hostile bands. There was also to be a line of strong points farther from the border, with a large force of Navajos and other Indian scouts who would catch any hostile who got through and keep out the gunrunners and whiskey sellers.[155]

In response to Crook's request for scouts, more than one hundred Navajo males turned out at Fort Wingate. The army enlisting officer stated, "I have always procured young healthy and finely made men. I have one old man [in each group] and he exerts a good influence over the younger men." The recruiters also wanted Navajos who in some degree understood Spanish or English.[156]

One Navajo Scout who took part in the Geronimo campaign was known as Hashkéiil Naabaah, "Wars About with Anger" (aka War Boy). He recalled his role in the Geronimo War in great detail.

The trouble started, according to War Boy, when a group of Apaches left their reservation at the time they were to get a beef ration. A party of soldiers and Navajo scouts was sent out to find the trail of the Apaches. They were able to find where the Apaches had been, and there was evidence

Above: Navajo scouts mounted and in formation, 1880s. *Ben Wittick, courtesy of Place of the Governors Photo Archive, New Mexico History Museum (NMHM/DCS), #016338.*

Left: Navajo scout Juan. *Ben Wittick, 1880s, courtesy of Place of the Governors Photo Archive, New Mexico History Museum (NMHM/DCS), #015948.*

that they had stolen some cattle and butchered them. The scouts and troops returned to the main army camp to report. The officers in charge wanted to attack the Apache camp, but the troops said that they were outnumbered and it would be folly to attempt an assault on the hostiles. Later, now with reinforcements, the soldiers and scouts again sought to find the trail of the Apaches. Soon they found that the Apaches had burned out a ranch and killed three stockmen and were moving toward the Mexican border. The main party of troops and scouts set up a base camp while War Boy and a small detail of cavalry continued the chase. After following the trail for several miles, they came upon the body of a white woman propped up against a century plant. The body of an infant was found nearby beside the trail. The troops followed the Apaches' trail until it was too dark to continue on and made camp for the night.

The next day, War Boy lost the trail in an area of lava rocks and grass. Although some horse tracks were finally found, they led in another direction. War Boy told the officer in command that it was perhaps a trail made by stockmen and was not the Apaches' trail. The officer wanted to go on, and so the patrol went on following the wrong trail.

After a few days, they began to run short of water for the men and the horses. Soon the horse of a soldier called Three Stripes died. Other horses were becoming too weak to carry soldiers, and the men had to walk. War Boy told the officer in charge, "Why are we hauling all these things on pack mules? Let's throw the packs away and let men who lost their horses ride on the mules." The officer at first disagreed, but War Boy was at last able to persuade him to leave the packs and allow the men to ride the mules.

As the troops continued their march, War Boy showed them how to peel off the outer layer of the yucca and chew the inner part. The men did this, and it helped them overcome thirst. At last, they found some water, and the men and horses drank. As the men rested, War Boy went to a hilltop and saw two Mexicans on horseback. He called to them, but they were afraid that he was an Apache and would not come close. Finally, he was able to tell them there were soldiers nearby, and with the help of the Mexicans, the troops were able to return to their base camp.

Soon after their return, War Boy and several other Navajo scouts again took the field with troops to find the fleeing Apaches. War Boy said that seven Navajos were with the army, but he recalled the names of only Yóool katl ni bida (Patchers Son), Ashiiké Yazhi (Little Boy) and Hoolyo.

As the detail marched on, the scouts were sent ahead of the soldiers, who followed a few miles behind. As he looked for signs in the trail, War Boy noticed several yucca cacti laid across the path with pieces of cooked meat woven through the Yucca leaves. War Boy knew this was an Apache trail marker. The marker may have told the location of a food cache. The scouts halted and waited for the troops to catch up. When War Boy reported the marker to the officer in charge, he cursed and had the troops march on.

Moving down the trail, the troops came to a valley where there was an Apache camp, but the people had moved on. Still farther on, they came to a blind canyon.

At this point in the story, War Boy tells of an agreement made with the Apaches and the scout Hoolyo sometime before; however, War Boy said he did not know of this agreement until much later. War Boy said that Hoolyo was told by an Apache that "when we may fight with the soldiers, you Navajos will ride through our ranks and then join us in the shooting.... Whenever we lay an ambush, we'll place two rocks, one upon the other."

When the scouts crossed the stream into the canyon, War Boy said he noticed Hoolyo was jittery. He knew what lay ahead. The scouts advanced into the canyon and waited for the soldiers. Then the scouts gave their horses to the soldiers and began to climb up the side of the canyon to gain a better view. As the Navajos made their way toward the rim to the canyon, suddenly an Apache woman began shouting loudly, followed by the sound of heavy gunfire. One of the scouts at the canyon rim was hit, fell back and rolled down the canyon side. The scouts raced down from the rim and took up a point near a washout on the canyon floor. The scouts began to return fire when they heard one of the Apaches cursing: "You Hoolyo from hell, we'll kill you for sure. We'll kill every last one of you." This, War Boy said, "was due to Hoolyo's agreement to join them. Which he did not do."

The fight continued all day long, and the troops lost every one of their horses. At last reinforcements came, and the Apaches moved off. War Boy reported that three Navajo scouts were killed and three were unhurt. He also said that he and Hoolyo had carried a wounded Navajo scout and a white soldier to safety.

When they got back to base, the officers were waiting for them, and they all joyfully shook hands. War Boy found his horse, which had escaped the fight, standing in the corral. He went up to his horse, pulled out his pollen bag and put some of it on the horse and in its mouth. Then War Boy prayed.[157]

General George Crook's line of defense and his aggressive campaigns into Mexico failed to check Apache raiders into the United States. In March 1883, Apache leader Chato with twenty-five warriors crossed into Arizona and New Mexico, destroying many homesteads and slaying settlers.

Navajo scout Charlie, Fort Wingate, 1880s. *Ben Wittick, courtesy of Place of the Governors Photo Archive, New Mexico History Museum (NMHM/DCS), #015933.*

In response, on May 1, Crook entered into Mexico with a force of Apache scouts determined to crush the Apache resistance. With the aid of an Apache scout named Peaches, Crook was able to locate Chato's camp in the Sierra Madre and launch an attack. Then the hostiles were ready to talk peace terms. Geronimo and other leaders spent a week talking with Crook and at last agreed to return to San Carlos. While most of the other Apache bands arrived at San Carlos in a timely manner, Geronimo's band did not arrive until March 1884, asking for peace. By the spring of 1885, Geronimo and other Apache leaders had grown angry over General Crook's ban on the making of tiswin (a beer-like alcoholic drink). The tension grew until May 1885, when Geronimo led forty-two men and ninety-two women and children into Mexico.[158]

During 1885, various Apache bands struck terror in both northern Mexico and the American Southwest. Some of these groups, known as Broncos or Renegades because they would not be confined to reservations, were under the leadership of Geronimo, and others were only loosely linked to him.[159]

These bands of Broncos were made up of various groups of Apaches, such as Ojo Calientes, Chiricahuas, Mescaleros and even a few Navajos. The Navajos who joined the Broncos may have done so because of their dissatisfaction with their current agent or a desire for the old life of freedom and raiding, or perhaps they had Apache in-laws.[160]

One raider leader was Ulzana, who had served as an army scout during the Nana campaign and was familiar with both the tactics of the military and Nana's skill in avoiding the Americans. During late fall and winter of 1885, his band swept across western New Mexico and eastern Arizona, attacking ranches and farms and the White Mountain Apache Reservation.

In November, they crossed from Mexico into New Mexico's Florida Mountains and fell upon a detachment of cavalry, which included both Navajo and Apache scouts. In the fight that followed, two Navajo scouts, one White Mountain Apache scout and one solider were killed. On November 24, the Broncos killed two employees of the Fort Apache Agency and then, angered when White Mountain Apaches refused to join the raid, set upon the White Mountain people. During this raid, it has been estimated that the raiders killed twenty White Mountain Apaches and kidnapped several young women, forcing them to join the raiders.[161]

The next stop on the raid was near Alma, New Mexico, where the raiders killed two civilians. Lieutenant Samuel Warren Fountain, with Troop C of the Eighth Cavalry from Fort Bayard, and ten Navajo scouts picked up the trail of the raiders and pursued them into the Mogollon Mountains. Major Biddle, with a force that included forty Navajo scouts, left his base camp at Horse Springs and moved to join Fountain. However, Fountain's Navajos located the Broncos' camp and were able to capture their supplies and several horses. But the raiders escaped.[162]

On December 10, the raiders attacked Lillie's Ranch on Clear Creek in New Mexico, killed the owner and a ranch hand and captured several horses. Fountain's scouts followed the raiders but lost the trail. With no hope of catching the Apaches and running short of supplies, Fountain elected to return to Fort Bayard. As Fountain was breaking camp on December 19, he found that his Navajo scouts were hesitant to leave the campsite. Fountain sent his wagons and an escort forward while he tried to persuade his scouts to join the caravan and take their posts at the head of the column. The wagons were not far down the trail when they were ambushed by Apaches. In this ambush, four troopers and army surgeon Dr. Maddox were killed. The Navajo scouts did advance to the fight, taking a position at the top of a hill, and opened fire on the hostiles, at which point the hostiles retreated. The Navajo scouts had saved the cavalry. Lieutenant Fountain wrote later in his report that "the Navajo Scouts did remarkable well [sic]."[163]

On December 26, Lieutenant David N. McDonald with M Troop, of the Fourth Cavalry, and another group of Navajo scouts joined Lieutenant Albert B. Scott, plus an additional fifty Navajo scouts. The combined force continued the pursuit of Ulzana's hostiles. But this group of scouts had had enough. With no supplies and their horses worn out, the scouts refused to go on. Lieutenant McDonald was unable to persuade the scouts to stay and reported that he was unable to follow the trail through rough and rocky country without the aid of scouts.[164]

The *New Mexico Gazette* reported the incident in its January 8, 1886 edition noting, with displeasure, that the military was afraid to use force to disarm the Navajos and allowed them to return to their reservation.[165] The *Clifton Clarion* of January 6, 1886, noted that Colonel Bradley was able to "sort out" the conflict and prevent any bloodshed between the soldiers and the scouts. The *Clarion* agreed with the *Gazette* that the Navajo scouts were not punished for mutiny in the field and that the army feared an incident could lead to a Navajo uprising. The *Clarion* noted, "It was a breach of military discipline but the circumstances with the Apaches and Navajo both at us, we should indeed be in a wretched plight."[166]

Navajo scout Jose Rayo had a different view of the incident: "We had trouble with the officers as they gave us nothing to eat for four days and we refused to go on until we had some food. That was all the trouble we ever had with officers."[167] Navajo scout Jake Segundo reported that the Navajos had their own horses, and they went over rocky country and were without water for days at a time. The scouts, Jake said, asked for shoes for the horses and to stay in camp for a few days and rest the animals. The officers refused, and several of the horses died. Jake went on to say that upon returning to Fort Wingate, the officers reported the trouble, and the superintendent asked questions about the trouble and spoke to the "headman" at Fort Wingate. After a meeting, those officers were removed, and another officer was placed in charge of scouts.[168]

There were some consequences for some of the scouts involved in the incident of December 26. Scouts Sergeant Jose Armijo and Privates Antonio and Nagle appeared before a military court at Fort Wingate in October 1886 and were found guilty of desertion. The three were sentenced to loss of pay and allowances and six months' confinement at hard labor and were dishonorably discharged from the army. However, a review court at Fort Whipple, Arizona, remitted the confinement at hard labor.[169]

In December, Ulzana's Broncos crossed into Mexico. In the raid they had covered more than one thousand miles, killed thirty-eight people and captured nearly three hundred horses and mules.[170]

To end such raids in the United States, Crook again led troops into Mexico and, after a costly campaign, was able to reach an agreement with Geronimo at Canyon de los Embudos on March 25, 1886. The hostile Apaches agreed to surrender and to be confined in the eastern United States for two years before being returned to San Carlos. But after Crook left for Fort Bowie to report to his superior, General Phillip Sheridan, Geronimo led twenty men and thirteen women back into the Sierra Madre.[171]

Following yet another failure by Crook to end the Apache resistance, General Sheridan allowed General Crook to resign his command in Arizona and replaced him with Brigadier General Nelson A. Miles.

Because of his own views and the views of his commander, General Sheridan, who, due to the Cibicue mutiny, did not trust the loyalty of Apache scouts, General Miles planned to rely less on Indian scouts than did General Crook. Miles distrusted the Chiricahua and Ojo Caliente Apache scouts because he thought that they had more loyalty to their renegade relatives than to the army. In their place, he enlisted Indian scouts from tribes or bands that were antagonistic to the Chiricahuas, a majority of which were from the White Mountain Apaches and the Navajos.[172]

Following this policy, General Miles authorized the enlistment of 150 Navajo scouts. The *Weekly Commercial Herald* of Jackson, Mississippi, reported that Lieutenant Stanton of General Miles's staff was in New Mexico enlisting Navajos to act as scouts.[173] Stanton's enlistment of Navajos from May to October 1886 would be the largest number of Navajos enrolled into the United States Army until World War I. During this time, two Navajo women, Mexicana Chiquito (aka Nal Kai) and Muchacha, were enlisted as scouts in the Twentieth Infantry Regiment. These two were the first women

Navajo Scouts During the Apache Wars

Left: Old Navajo scout Jake Segundo. He served five enlistments as a scout and later became the Navajo police chief at Crownpoint, New Mexico. He was the nephew of Mariano. *Courtesy of Navajo Nation Museum, Window Rock, Arizona.*

Below: General Miles on horseback early 1900s. *Courtesy of Wikimedia Commons.*

Old Navajo scout Apachito. Was born in 1846 and went as a child to Fort Sumner. *Courtesy of Navajo Nation Museum, Window Rock, Arizona.*

to be enlisted to serve in a combat unit in the United States Army.[174]

Newspapers across the Southwest questioned the wisdom of arming and training so many Native Americans. The Arizona press expressed the fear of many western settlers that the army was far too trustful of the Navajos. The *Arizona Silverbelt* published an editorial in June 1886 asking General Miles to use extreme caution in the enlisting of Navajos as scouts. The editor said that many Navajos may be friendly with the hostile Apaches.[175]

The mistrust of Indian scouts was apparent when Lieutenant O'Brien and eleven men of the Eighth Cavalry, with six Navajo scouts, were sent to Clifton, Arizona, to arrest a civilian who was charged with killing and scalping an Indian. When O'Brien reached Clifton, an angry mob surrounded the patrol. O'Brien later reported that his men were lucky to get out of town alive.[176]

Fear and mistrust of Indian scouts was not always the case. The *Black Range* reported that about fifty Navajo scouts, well mounted and under the command of Lieutenant Hall, arrived at the town of Camp Fairview, New Mexico, and that the Indians were of peculiar interest to the ranchers along the valley, as well as to the town people. The paper noted that the Indians were successful in selling a number of trinkets, bracelets and saddle blankets to the citizens. The scouts camped near the town for two days, even taking part in footraces with locals before leaving for Fort Cummings to await orders.[177]

The full enlistment of Navajos at Fort Wingate was three companies of scouts with fifty members each under Captain B.H. Rogers. Company A was led by Lieutenant O'Brien, Company B was led by Lieutenant Charles Gatewood, with Jose Chavez as first sergeant, and Company C was led by Lieutenant Hall.[178]

In 1886, Lieutenant Charles Gatewood, a noted leader of Apache scouts, was assigned to Fort Wingate to take command of a company of Navajo scouts. Gatewood did not want the Navajo assignment and grew frustrated with his unit's slow pace in taking the field due to the government not

Navajo Scouts During the Apache Wars

Navajo scouts the Pedro brothers. *Ben Wittick, courtesy of Place of Governors Photo Archive, New Mexico History Museum (NMHM/DCS), #015709.*

Left: Captain Benjamin H. Rogers of the Thirteenth Infantry and Navajo scout Largo, Fort Wingate. *Ben Wittick, 1880s, courtesy of Place of Governors Photo Archive, New Mexico History Museum (NMHM/DCS), #015717.*

Below: Apache scouts at Fort Wingate. *Courtesy of National Archives and Records, Washington, D.C., #111-SC-87797.*

delivering weapons in a timely manner. Gatewood, at a low place in his personal life and in his career and missing his Apache scouts command, noted that he found Navajo scouts to be "Coffee Coolers" and not as effective as Apaches.[179]

Miles set about developing a force of proven "Indian fighters" in the regular army, sending them on search-and-destroy missions to kill or capture as many of the hostiles as possible. He also planned to work in conjunction with Mexican forces to keep Geronimo and his allies on the move, not allowing them to rest until they were all dead or had surrendered unconditionally.

For the summer campaign of 1886, General Miles amassed a force of 5,000 cavalry and infantry regular troops, 500 Apache scouts and 150 Navajo scouts. He organized his forces into flying columns of cavalry supported by infantry and kept them in touch with one another through an extensive network of heliograph stations. While in Mexico, this force was supported by more than 1,000 troops of the Mexican army accompanied by Tarahumara Indian scouts.[180]

Several Navajo scouts recalled the summer of 1886 and related their stories to U.S. Pension Office officials some thirty years later.

General Miles in the field with staff. *Courtesy of Library of Congress.*

Old Navajo scout Pala Cosa. He served in the Apache War of 1886. At first, he was denied a pension because he was not listed on the enlistment roles, but he was eventually granted a pension in 1925. *Courtesy of Navajo Nation Museum, Window Rock, Arizona.*

Scout Pala Cosa, who served in Hall's Company C, remembered, "In 1886, I was with the company when they went down to Zuni, then we went to Horse Springs and our company stayed there four days and nights. Then we went straight over the hills to the Mexican border line and there we camped for some weeks, then we started back to Fort Wingate by the same route, stopping at Horse Springs, then to Fort Wingate where we were discharged."[181]

Scout Pinto (Assaloi Yazzi) reported that he was with Company C with Lieutenant Hall and was sent to Fort Cummings and then with Lieutenant Buck and Company B to scout in the Alma Mountains. Both of these companies, Pinto said, were part of General Miles's net to catch Apaches who were in Mexico and Arizona.[182]

Scout Jake Segundo of Company A reported a longer march. After reaching the Mexican border, Lieutenant O'Brien directed his scouts to go west but not to cross into Mexico. The scouts went 30 or so miles along the border line but found nothing. Stopping at a ranch, a cowboy told them that he had seen some Apaches, and O'Brien took Jake and nine other scouts into Mexico to go after them. For two days, they tracked the Apaches but did not catch them. On the third day, they returned to the American side of the border, where they had left the others. The whole company stayed in camp for two days and then moved to a new location. Captain Rogers, who was in charge of this part of the campaign, reported that troops under his command had scouted the Baca Grande Mountains in Mexico, but heavy rains made it impossible to follow any tracks. Rogers said his troops had covered 175 miles in Mexico.[183]

Pushed deeper and deeper into Mexico and denied the chance to rest or resupply, by the late summer of 1886 the Broncos were ready to talk peace.

Lieutenant Charles Gatewood, happy at last to command a patrol of Apache scouts, was in pursuit of Geronimo. Gatewood and his scouts had camped for the night when they were contacted by two Apache women,

Lozen, the sister of Victorio, and Dah-Tes-Te. The women informed Gatewood that Geronimo wanted to talk. Gatewood agreed to a meeting. The next morning, he set out for Geronimo's camp accompanied by the women and two Apache scouts, Martine and Kayitah.[184]

On August 24, Gatewood reached Geronimo's camp. At the meeting between the two, Geronimo asked for the peace terms that had been offered by Crook in March at Canyon Embudos, namely that they would be reunited with their families and after a two-year imprisonment in the East be returned to San Carlos. Gatewood refused these terms, telling Geronimo that he must surrender and that he and his followers would be sent to Florida. A return to the Southwest would be up to officials in Washington. At first, Geronimo refused, saying he would fight on, but he changed his mind after conferring with his followers and agreed to surrender if his band were allowed to return to San Carlos and live with the rest of the Chiricahuas.

Geronimo, Lozen and other Apaches being removed by train from Arizona. *Courtesy of National Anthropological Archives, Washington, D.C.*

Navajo Scouts During the Apache Wars

Above: Apache POWs at Fort Bowie, Arizona. *Courtesy of National Anthropological Archives, Washington, D.C.*

Left: Navajo scouts leaving Fort Wingate. *Henry T. Hiester, 1872–78, courtesy of Place of the Governors Photo Archive, New Mexico History Museum (NMHM/DCS), #037963.*

Gatewood then told him the news that all the Chiricahuas had already been sent to Florida. Geronimo, shocked by this news, then agreed to meet with General Miles at Skeleton Canyon, and on September 4, he surrendered.[185]

After Geronimo's surrender, his band was escorted to Fort Bowie. At Fort Bowie Station, Geronimo, Nana, Lozen and other leaders were sent by railroad to Florida via Texas. The remainder of Geronimo's band and other Apaches, including Apache scouts and their families, some 350 people, were marched to Holbrook, Arizona, to be placed on trains to Florida and Alabama. Troops from several forts and Navajo scouts patrolled the route to Holbrook, as well as the railway route, until the Apaches were out of Arizona.[186]

According to Navajo scout Jake Segundo, he said his officer told the scouts, "Go back to Fort Wingate. We do not need you any more," and they were led back from Arizona by their officers and one old Navajo. Jake said his company of scouts was mustered out on October 11 and 13, 1886. Navajo scout Choski summed up the Navajo view of the Geronimo War, proudly observing, "I was a scout just one summer and we captured the whole Geronimo outfit.[187]

Chapter 10

VARIOUS ROLES OF NAVAJO SCOUTS

The Navajo scouts' role was not only that of a warrior but also as a peacekeeper. An important function of Indian scouts was to serve as a mediator between the United States and the Indian communities. This role was often at the local level, working with individuals and groups to keep them from joining more militant factions on the reservation.

In his autobiography, *Navajo Blessingway Singer*, Frank Mitchell discussed how the scouts helped to keep peace on the Navajo Nation. The government, Mitchell observed, did not trust the Navajo people very much, so they wanted to get someone to come out to the people and serve as a peacemaker. He cited the action of Navajo scout "Son of the Late Little Blacksmith," who was from the Eastern Navajo area. Mitchell said that when any trouble happened and the troops were sent out, Little Blacksmith would be one of the scouts to go because with his experience and skill, he was able to explain to the people what the rules were. In later years, Little Blacksmith became a peace officer and guide.

Mitchell said that scouts like Jeff King, Old Man Short Hair and Mitchell's brother, Charlie, picked up a lot of ideas about the rules the Navajos were to follow and could explain these to the people. Headmen, Mitchell said, asked scouts to come and meet with the people to keep the peace. Mitchell said that he learned to talk to the people from these meetings between the people and the scouts. "This is how I learned about the white man's law," said Mitchell.[188]

Navajo Scouts During the Apache Wars

Above: Captain Allen Smith and Navajo scouts at Fort Wingate, 1880s. *Christian Barthelmess, courtesy of Beinecke Library Yale University, #16174285.*

Right: Old Navajo scout Charlie Mitchell. He became a community leader and a Navajo policeman. *Courtesy of Navajo Nation Museum, Window Rock, Arizona.*

Navajo Scouts During the Apache Wars

Navajo scouts Charlie Mitchell and Atta-Kai-Bi-Za-in Fort Wingate, 1884. *Ben Wittick, courtesy of Place of the Governors Photo Archive, New Mexico History Museum (NMHM/DCS), #015726.*

Navajo Scouts During the Apache Wars

The principal function of the army in the West was to keep the peace. This, in many cases, involved the removal of settlers encroaching on Indian lands. Most of the problems in the Fort Wingate area had their roots with these disputes. Captain Kerr had to deal with this on February 13, 1887, when he wrote from Manuelito, New Mexico, "I will leave tomorrow morning with a detachment for Houck's Tank, Bennett Ranch and the vicinity of the recent disturbance between certain citizens and the Navajo Indians." The disturbance started when a local Navajo named Hosteen Chee found a horse belonging to the ranch owner Bennett and returned the animal to the ranch. However, a cowboy on the Bennett ranch, named Palmer, thought that Chee had stolen the horse, and with the aid of two other cowboys named Lockhart and King, he went looking for Chee. Finding a group of Navajo hogans, which they thought belonged to Hosteen Chee, they fired into the hogans, killing two Navajo men. Before dying, the Navajos were able to return fire, and Palmer died during the fighting. Lockhart and King retreated from the scene after firing more shots.

When Kerr arrived at Houck's Tank, he sent two Navajo scouts, one of whom he noted spoke English, to meet with several hundred Navajos who had gathered in the hills northeast of Houck's Tank. The scouts were able to prevent the affair from becoming a violent conflict between the local settlers. The local Navajo headman, Dewetnich, sent two of his men to help search for Lockhart and King. Captain Kerr reported later that the remains of Lockhart and King were found some distance from Hosteen Chee's hogan, hatcheted by some unknown party.[189]

The San Juan River Valley was an area of conflict between settlers and Navajo stockmen. In June 1887, Lieutenant Scott—with a mixed force of infantry, cavalry and two Navajo scouts—left Fort Wingate for the San Juan region. Upon reaching the area, the local Navajos asked Scott to remove the settlers who were building houses and bring livestock onto the Navajo lands. Scott initially informed the Navajos that they were to "let the settlers alone" in order to keep the peace. However, further investigation revealed that three groups of settlers were trespassing on Navajo land, and they refused to move unless forcibly ejected. Finding no other solution to the problem, Scott ordered his troops to remove the trespassers.

This action, and others by the army protecting Diné Bikéyah (the Navajo Nation) against incursions by settlers, along with the use of Navajo scouts as translators to learn the Navajo side of conflicts, helped shape a favorable opinion of the military in the minds of the Navajo people. The

A group of Mormon settlers, 1890s. *Ben Wittick, courtesy of Place of the Governors Photo Archive, New Mexico History Museum (NMHM/DCS), #015683.*

Navajos were beginning to look on the military as a protector and advocate and not as an occupier.[190]

Navajo scouts as peacemakers involved them in disputes outside the Navajo Nation. In 1914, a conflict between settlers and Paiutes led to violence in southern Utah. A sheepherder named Juan Chacon was found dead, and his murder was blamed on Tsenegar (aka Everett Hatch), a Paiute related to Old Polk, a Paiute leader who had resisted settlers squatting on his peoples' land. The settlers formed a posse made up of volunteers under the leadership of U.S. Marshal Aquila Nebeker to hunt down Tsenegar.[191] In February 1915,

NAVAJO SCOUTS DURING THE APACHE WARS

Fort Wingate, New Mexico, 1873. *Timothy H. O'Sullivan, courtesy of National Archives and Records, Washington, D.C., #106-WB-323.*

they attacked Old Polk's camp. Tsenegar was not in the camp, nor did the people know why they were being attacked. The predawn fighting resulted in the death of two Indians and one settler. After the fight, known as the Battle of Cottonwood Gulch, the Paiutes fled. The settlers of southern Utah requested military protection, and a military force under General Hugh L. Scott was sent from Fort Wingate to Bluff, Utah, to restore order.

Meanwhile, Tsenegar sought the counsel of Louisa Weatherill, the wife of John Weatherill, a well-respected trader in the northern Navajo Nation. She advised him to turn himself in at the Ute Mountain Ute Agency. Tsenegar, fearing that no one would believe that he was innocent, sought refuge in a more isolated area of the Four Corners.[192]

General Scott's goal was to end this dispute in a peaceful manner. He did not want to see any more bloodshed, and he did not want an escalation into an Indian war, not in 1915. General Scott at first requested Tsenegar and those aiding him to come into his headquarters and talk. But they refused. Then Scott himself, unarmed and accompanied only by an orderly and two Navajo scouts, journeyed to the Paiute camp. After several days of discussion, Tsenegar and three others rode into Bluff, Utah, and gave themselves up.

NAVAJO SCOUTS DURING THE APACHE WARS

General Hugh L. Scott.
Courtesy of Wikimedia Commons.

General Scott escorted the prisoners to Salt Lake City to turn them over to federal authorities.[193] Tsenegar and his codefendants were later tried by a federal court in Denver and found innocent.

In addition to scouting, native auxiliaries also performed service as police, freeing regulars for other duties and preventing unnecessary army/Indian collisions.[194] The Navajo scouts also served as a police force, much like their predecessor, the Navajo cavalry. They often dealt with Navajos who still followed the old habit of raiding. They were, however, in some cases called on to deal with crimes by non-Indians. One such event took place in November 1897.

The High Five Gang from Arizona robbed a stagecoach and was chased by a local posse. In a place on the New Mexico/Arizona border known as Black Jack Canyon, the posse caught up with the gang, and in the gunfight that followed, the gang's leader, Willian Christian, was killed. The remainder of the gang escaped and made its way to New Mexico, where the members hoped to have better luck.

Bob Christian, Willian's brother and the new leader of the High Five (now reduced to three), planned to rob the Atlantic and Pacific eastbound train to Albuquerque. On the evening of November 6, 1897, the gang boarded the Eastbound no. 2 in Grants, New Mexico. When the train stopped for water a short distance from town, they commandeered the train. Most of the train crew escaped when the outlaws fired warning shots. The train's fireman, Henry Able, was not as lucky and was forced to uncouple the train cars and drive the engine a mile or so farther east. The outlaws found that the train's express agent had locked the express car door before he escaped. The gang blew the door off and, once inside, also blasted open the safe, taking more than $100,000 in cash and gold. True to the code of the Old West, they gave Henry Able a bottle of whiskey for his trouble and rode off into the night.[195]

Rio Grande Railroad engine at water tank,1903. *Courtesy of Place of Governors Photo Archive, New Mexico History Museum (NMHM/DCS), #98222.*

The next morning, a posse arrived from Albuquerque and requested the aid of Navajo scouts from Fort Wingate. The scouts, under the leadership of Jeff King, a noted tracker from the Geronimo campaign, led the posse to where the outlaws had stopped to rest near Fence Lake, New Mexico. In the gun battle that followed, one gang member was killed, one was captured and another was able to escape. A lawman and a Navajo scout were also killed. But somewhere along the route of their escape, the surviving members of the High Five Gang hid their loot, and to this day, it has not been recovered.[196]

Navajo scouts were also called out to deal with incidents on the Navajo Nation. Agent to the Navajo Ruben Perry had unwisely attempted to make an arrest concerning a rape charge against a Navajo man from the Chinle area in Arizona. Charles Cousins, the local trader, was able to rescue Perry from an angry crowd of the man's relatives. Charles Cousins was a veteran of the Sixth Cavalry and had served with the Navajo scouts in the Geronimo campaign. He had learned enough of the Navajo language from his time at Fort Wingate that he went into the trading business after his discharge.

Because of his language skills and good sense, he was often called to interpret and help settle local disputes.

Cousins himself would need help a few days after the Perry incident when his store and Sam Day's store at St. Michaels were broken into and a large amount of jewelry and pawn was stolen. When Cousins opened his store one morning, several Navajo men entered wearing bracelets that had been stolen a few days earlier. Cousins demanded that the jewelry be returned, but the men refused. Cousins took a pistol from under the counter and locked the trading post door, saying no one would leave until the jewelry was returned.

A tense day was spent in the locked store until a knock came at the door at dusk. Charles Cousins cautiously opened the door expecting to see more angry Navajos, but instead he was greeted by a cavalry trooper and a Navajo scout. The troops had been patrolling the area after the Perry Affair to make sure everything remained peaceful. Hearing about the trading post robberies, the patrol decided to check and make sure everything was all right. Before leaving the area, the troops arrested two of the ringleaders and collected many of the stolen items.[197]

Navajo scouts also served to support military discipline and help prevent friction between the military and towns boarding a military post. The *Albuquerque Daily Citizen* of June 26, 1900, reported that a cavalry trooper got a little too much "bug juice" in a Gallup saloon and was ordered back to Fort Wingate by Lieutenant Nichols. However, on the way back to the post, the drunken trooper passed out and fell off his mount. The next day, two Navajo scouts were sent out to recover the horse. They found the animal sixteen miles south of Gallup.[198]

At times, scouts were called out to deal with military crimes. The *Tombstone Epitaph* reported in May 1892 that Juan Marquez, a former Indian scout, had killed a Navajo woman four miles west of Fort Wingate. After committing the murder, Marquez fled south but was overtaken by a detail of Navajo scouts about twenty miles south of Gallup. When ordered to surrender, Marquez replied by shooting at the scouts, who returned fire and fatally wounded Marquez. His body was returned to Fort Wingate.[199]

Troops and scouts were also called out to enforce school attendance by native children. In November 1911, Colonel Hugh L. Scott and one hundred men of the Twelfth Cavalry, with Navajo scouts, began the removal of Hopi children to the government school at Hotevilla.[200]

An important role of Indian scouts was to serve as guides to military officers and other prominent persons. The Navajo scouts were no exception to this task. In 1887, Second Lieutenant John J. Pershing was assigned to

Navajo Scouts During the Apache Wars

Navajo scout with officers on a hunting trip at Nutria near Zuni, New Mexico, 1880s. *Christian Barthelmess, courtesy of Beinecke Library Yale University, #16174294.*

Fort Wingate. At that time, the post was staffed with five troops of the Sixth Cavalry, two companies of the Ninth Infantry and one company of Navajo Indian scouts. Lieutenant Pershing chose one of the scouts, a Carlisle Indian Schools graduate, to guide him on a sightseeing expedition to the Grand Canyon, a trip that Pershing thoroughly enjoyed.[201]

Scouts also served as hunting guides for officers and visitors to Fort Wingate. The Zuni Mountains near Fort Wingate were noted by several officers as an excellent area for hunting for turkey, deer, bear and elk. Navajo scouts also served as guides and interpreters to a diverse group of scholars, visitors and hobbyists assigned to military installations. The scouts provided assistance to Dr. Washington Matthews, who began the first systematic study of the Navajo language and culture. Scouts also worked with frontier photographers Christian Barthelmess, Ben Wittick and Julian Scott.

Scouts worked as laborers at military post building quarters, developing roads, caring for livestock and tending gardens. Such work was common for all enlisted men on the frontier.[202] Scouts were also able to supplement their pay by hunting and fishing and selling their catch to the officers' mess. Some scouts even sold arts and crafts to military personnel and civilians.[203]

Chapter 11

OLD SCOUTS

On March 4, 1917, Congress passed legislation to provide a pension to the veterans of the Indian Wars, fought from January 1859 to January 1891. In addition to the veterans themselves, the act provided for the widows of veterans as long as they were married to the veteran before the passage of the act and had not remarried.

Proof of service was an important feature of the act. Because of the practice of short-term service during the various Indian campaigns, the requirements for a pension were made broad. Veterans of the Indian Wars must have reached the age of sixty-two and had served for at least thirty days in a campaign against hostile Indians.

Proof of service was to be based on War and Treasury Department records. If no record were found from these sources, a veteran might establish proof from local muster rolls. An important provision of the act was "[t]hat the want of a certificate of discharge shall not deprive any applicant of the benefits of this Act."[204]

Native soldiers, known as scouts, were included in this act and were able to gain a pension if they were able to prove their service.

During the 1920s, Navajo veterans of the Indian Wars began to file applications for pensions. Agency superintendent Samuel Franklin Stacher of the Pueblo Bonito Agency (later the Eastern Navajo Agency) was instrumental in assisting old scouts in gaining a pension. Stacher wrote many letters in support of scout claims to the United States Pension Office in Washington, D.C.

NAVAJO SCOUTS DURING THE APACHE WARS

Eastern Navajo agent S.F. Stacher, pension office investigator C.R. Frank and old scouts, Crownpoint, New Mexico, 1926. *Courtesy of National Anthropological Archives, Washington, D.C., #NMNH-02277400.*

The application process was quite complicated and time-consuming. The process began with a cover letter from Stacher to the commissioner of pensions, routed through the Office of Indian Affairs. The application would include a statement from Stacher that the applicant was a member of the Navajo tribe and over sixty-two years of age. Included in the application were several statements by scouts who had served with the applicant. These statements discussed the campaigns in which the scouts took part, dates of enlistment and discharge, unit served in and name of a company officer if recalled. These statements were signed by the old scouts, usually by thumb print, and notarized by Stacher or an agency clerk. Yet another document was a form titled "Declaration for Survivor's Pension-Indian Wars." This document contained all the details of the scout's service, a physical description of the scout and his current address and occupation. Also noted were the name of his wife or wives and dependent children. Once the scout's application reached the Indian Bureau in Washington, D.C., it was reviewed and sent to the United States Pension Office.

If there was a question concerning the scouts' application, C.R. Frank, a pension office investigator based in Denver, Colorado, would make a follow-up inquiry. Frank made several visits to the agency office in Crownpoint, New Mexico, to interview old scouts and review records with Agent Stacher. In a December 28, 1925 letter to Stacher from Frank, he stated that he needed to meet with seven pension applicants to gain more information about their claims. He also noted that widows' claims were difficult to understand because his office had little knowledge about Navajo marriage customs.

It is clear from the many letters exchanged between the two men that they developed a friendly relationship. In the letter on December 28, Frank closed with a brief note about his Christmas holiday and how he has a Victrola and might listen to the music he likes rather than having to hear jazz on the radio.[205]

Stacher clearly became frustrated with the long and slow process of gaining the old scouts' pensions. In a letter to the pension office on July 10, 1925, Stacher complained, "May we urge that this and the numerous other cases now before your office be expedited as these men are all getting old and they should be given this compensation at the earliest possible date."[206]

Once the pension was approved, an "Individual Indian Moneys" account was established in the scout's name at the agency office. Funds would flow from the United States Treasury to the agency office, and those funds would be placed in the each scout's pension account. The scouts received a monthly stipend check to the scout themselves or to a bank account. These payments ranged from $20 to $50 per month for scouts and $20 to $30 per month to widows. In some cases, as much as $23,000 was paid in back pension. Most of the money, according to S.F. Stacher's unpublished autobiography, went to buy livestock.[207] In many cases, a check was sent to the scout's local trading post. Stacher's file at the Navajo Nation Archives is filled with letters from old scouts asking that their check be sent to various trading posts. There were also letters from traders asking when a scout's check would arrive, as he had a large debt at the post and his credit would be cut off if not paid soon. Trader's letters also named old scouts in the community who had not applied for a pension and needed help in gaining one.[208]

It was the responsibility of the Bureau of Indian Affairs and the local agent, in this case S.F. Stacher, to keep track of the disbursement of these funds and to make necessary adjustments as time progressed and as the scouts underwent life changes. Old scouts could make claims for an increase in benefits if they could prove a service-related injury. When a scout claimed a service-related disability, it was up to Stacher to arrange a physical examination with a doctor and refer the results to the pension office. Stacher also used eyewitness reports of old scouts who served with the claimant and included their statements with the claim request.[209]

The death of an old scout opened up a process of requesting funeral costs and filing a claim for the widow. After the knowledge of the old scout's death

Navajo Scouts During the Apache Wars

Left: Old Navajo scout Frank Taylor. Born in 1864, possibly at Fort Sumner, he served as a scout in 1886 and 1891. *Courtesy of Navajo Nation Museum, Window Rock, Arizona.*

Below: Old Navajo scout Juarito Gonzales. He became a community leader and a medicine man. *Courtesy of Navajo Nation Museum, Window Rock, Arizona.*

was received, Stacher would contact the pension office to stop payment and begin to sort out the claims of the scout's heirs. Navajo marriage customs were a mystery for the pension office, and most marriages were listed as "Common Law." Many old scouts were widowers and had remarried. The key factor in the second wife getting any benefits was whether or not she was married to the scout before the legal cutoff date of March 4, 1917. In the place of marriage documents, Stacher used testimony of family members, friends and, in many cases, a local Indian trader who knew the deceased and his/her family well. Children who might receive benefits were also a matter to be reviewed by Agent Stacher, who used the testimony of local people to support the families' claims.[210]

From 1873 to the 1890s, an estimated 400 Navajos served as scouts, most of these coming from the eastern section of the Navajo Nation. From the 1920s to the early 1960s, more than 125 Navajo scouts and their spouses received pensions. The impact of the old scouts' pensions and the pensions for widows and children had a great effect on the Navajo economy and the economy of the region. Local historian Geraldine Tietjen said of the village of Ramah and the Ramah Navajos that the only people to have any money during the Depression were the two or three old Indian scouts who received a pension of about thirty dollars per month for having served in the Apache War.[211] Indian traders were active in helping old scouts secure a pension because their customers had a monthly cash flow with which to pay bills for the whole family.

Navajo historian Jennifer Nez Denetdale wrote that the pension income of her great-great-grandfather Dagah Chii (aka Pete Dougal Chee) was vital to the family. When he died in 1942, the family lost an important source of income. She went on to state, "Given the context of the times, it must have been a hardship indeed for the family to lose this income. A glimpse of Navajo life during this period indicates that, as with many other extended families, Dagha Chii was responsible for several generations."[212]

Pete Dug a chee Bekis. After service as a scout, he became a community leader. *Courtesy of Navajo Nation Museum, Window Rock, Arizona.*

Left: Indian Wars medal, reverse. *Right*: Indian Wars medal, obverse. *Courtesy of Wikimedia Commons.*

Agent S.F. Stacher was also a promoter of the Navajo scout legacy. He was instrumental in scouts receiving the Federal Indian Wars Campaign medal, which was authorized by Congress in 1907 and was issued to veterans into the 1960s. Stacher arranged old scouts to be photographed wearing their medals, and he took fifty old scouts to the 1925 Gallup Inter-Tribal Ceremonial.[213]

Chapter 12

ECONOMIC FACTORS

The Navajo economy had been destroyed by the Navajo campaign of 1863–64 and the years spent at Fort Sumner. After their return to the Navajo homeland in 1868, the government issued rations and livestock provided to the families; however, this was not enough to produce a new and sustainable economy. The old "raid and trade" economy could not be revived without antagonizing the government, and this was something that Navajos wanted to avoid. As historian Robert C. Collman noted, "Navajos were not about to embark upon large scale raiding which would amount to open warfare with the Americans."[214]

In 1872, efforts were made by Navajo leaders and the United States military to stop raiding and to return any stolen livestock to their owners. Clearly something new had to be developed. If there could be no raiding, then herding, weaving and trading needed to be developed to take its place. At this same time, the use of money began to work its way into the Navajos' notion of wealth. Money as something of value was not new to the Navajos. Geronimo told his biographer, S.M. Barrett, that the Apaches learned the value of money from the Navajos.[215]

The employment by the army of Navajo scouts introduced a wage-based cash flow into the Navajo economy. The wage of thirteen dollars per month provided a scout and family a steady income for a six-month enlistment, with an opportunity to reenlist. This regular pay and benefits of military service for the scout and family was a major motivator for enlistment. Navajo historian Jennifer Nez Denetdale stated that Navajos first served to

Navajo scouts waiting to be paid at Fort Wingate 1886. *U.S. Army Signal Corps, courtesy of Place of the Governors Photo Archive, New Mexico History Museum (NMHM/DCS), #028535.*

support their families.[216] In later years, the income from military pensions for scout veterans and their spouses, about thirty dollars per month, became an important source of money to many families.

The impact of the scout wages and pensions may be reviewed by looking at R.C. Collman's master's thesis, "Navajo Scouts, 1873–1895." He estimated that 30 percent of Navajo males served as scouts during the period of the Apache Wars. He further stated that the majority of these scouts lived within a radius of fifty miles from Fort Wingate. The wages drawn during time of service and the pensions of veterans and their survivors had a dynamic impact on the Navajo economy, as reflected by the efforts of Indian traders to enroll scouts veterans into the pension system on the economy of the region.[217] It was not until railroad employment and its pension system and the WPA that a wage-based system would so heavily influence the Navajo economy again.

Chapter 13

SOCIAL AND CULTURAL FACTORS

The Treaty of 1868 placed the protection of the Navajo people in the hands of the United States Army. Before the Navajo War of 1863–64, protecting the people was the role of Navajo youth under the leadership of a local headman (Naat'aánii). The role of protector was of great importance in the Navajo culture. Young Navajos were taught to imitate the "Hero Twins" known as Born of Water (Tóbájíshchíní) and Enemy Slayer (Nayeé Neizghání), the male children of Changing Woman (Adsdzaá Nádleehí) and the Sun (Jóhonaáei).[218] The twins were brought up in hiding, but when they were discovered by spies for the enemy, they had to seek their father. Because their mother would not tell them the name of their father, they had no idea who to look for. Fortunately, they met Spider Woman (Náashjéii Asdzaá), who told them that the Sun is their father and gave them a charm that would help get them safely to Jóhonaáei's dwelling place. Upon reaching their father's home and after many tests, the twins were given weapons to defeat the enemy. The Hero Twins were now charged with making the world safe for the Navajo people, and to do this they had to destroy the many enemy monsters that were killing the people.[219]

These enemy monsters were created by the Navajos themselves due to their misdeeds of greed and lust, putting the world out of balance.[220] The deeds of the twins were the basis for many healing and protection ceremonies to restore *Hozho* (a state of continual good health, harmony, peace, beauty, balance and positive events in the lives of the people).[221]

Navajo Scouts During the Apache Wars

Protection from enemies was important to the Navajos. Navajo educator and author Ruth Roessell noted that Navajos have always felt that they are alone in the world and beset, besieged and surrounded by enemies.[222]

The Navajos who enlisted as scouts took on the role of protectors of the people and sought to restore *Hozho*. These men became scouts because they were Navajo. They did not seek personal glory. Navajos did not count coup (the act of touching an enemy in battle to prove bravery). They sought to preserve, protect, defend and revive their institutions.[223]

The questions may be asked: How could these Navajos join the U.S. military so soon after the Navajo War and Fort Sumner? Was not the United States the greatest monster of all?[224]

Many Navajos of the nineteenth century placed the blame for the Navajo War and the Long Walk on a small group of Navajos known as Ladrones, who raided and, by this action, brought about conflict.[225] The Ladrones, according to Colonel E.R.S. Canby of the Nineteenth Infantry and command officer of Fort Defiance, were the most warlike and desperate men of the Navajo Nation. They were the cause of much of the troubles between the New Mexicans and the Navajos. Canby did note that the New Mexicans also raided the Navajos, taking women and children as well as livestock. He estimated that in 1861, New Mexicans held more than 1,500 Navajos as slaves.[226]

Navajos at Fort Sumner (Bosque Redondo, Hwéeldi) in front of ration house, 1860s. *U.S. Army Signal Corps, courtesy of Place of the Governors Photo Archive, New Mexico History Museum (NMHM/DCS) #044516.*

Bad events, the Navajos said, came from bad actions. Harmony and beauty could only be restored by good actions—actions that would protect the Navajo people and restore *Hozho*. The Americans had damaged the Navajos, but the true cause of this damage was the violations of the "Navajo Way."[227]

There are many stories of how conflict began between the Navajos and their neighbors. One such allegory is called "Beginning of the Enemies." This parable relates that a Navajo leader called Na-Ta-Dzil (Chief Mountain) traveled from Dzil Náoodilii (Huerfano Mesa), a place sacred to the Navajos, to Coyote Canyon to warn the people about the consequences of their actions. He arrived during a large gathering for an Enemy Way Ceremony (Nidaa) and told the people that they must stop stealing horse and sheep from the Mexicans. The people ignored him and kept on dancing and singing. Angry, Na-Ta-Dzil rode to a pile of ashes and told the people that "even the bushes and stones around here will turn into their enemies now." The people continued to ignore him. But his predictions came true. The Navajos, due to their wrong actions, made enemies of their neighbors the Apaches, Ute, Mexican, Spanish and Puebloans.[228]

The Hwéeldi (Fort Sumner) experience notwithstanding, the Navajos never felt that they had been defeated by the United States.[229] During the 1840s and 1850s, the Navajos maintained their independence of the American military and government. Until the Navajo War of 1863–64, the Navajo military organization proved itself effective in both offensive and defensive warfare. At Fort Sumner, Navajo leaders were able to hold the people together by reinforcing their cultural values. When the Navajos returned home in 1868, they were psychologically undefeated and, in many ways, more united as a people than ever before.[230]

The Navajos looked on their military experience as a way to learn all they could from the Americans and to use that knowledge to their best advantage.

Chapter 14

THE LEGACY OF THE NAVAJO SCOUTS

In June 2018, Peterson Zah, former Navajo Nation president, remarked at the unveiling of the original Navajo Treaty of 1868 at the Navajo Nation Museum in the Navajo capital of Window Rock, Arizona, that the piece of land granted to the Navajos in the treaty was about 1 million acres and that the Navajo Nation has expanded far beyond that original boundary. Zah stated further that the Navajo population in 1868 was about 8,000 people and that today that number is 300,000 Navajo citizens. Former president Zah attributed this growth in both land base and population to the resilience, imagination and cooperation of the Navajo people.[231]

Much of the credit for the success of the Navajos in keeping much of their ancestral lands and not becoming involved in any costly conflict with the United States belongs to Mariano.

Mariano was the Naat'aánii (leader) of the eastern non-treaty boundary (public domain) Navajos located in what is now known as the Checkerboard. The 1868 Navajo treaty set aside a reservation in the middle of the Navajos' much larger homeland.[232] These non-treaty lands had been the home to Navajos for centuries, and upon their return, they resettled their former homes. This resettlement was uneasy because the Navajos were not guaranteed this area by treaty. To make matters worse, a strip of land one hundred miles wide was opened to support the construction of a transcontinental railroad.[233]

Mariano was astute in seeing the danger of the loss of these lands to settlers, some of whom had already established themselves and were beginning to look on the Navajos as trespassers.[234]

Navajo Scouts During the Apache Wars

Navajo leader Mariano. *Ben Wittick, 1880s, courtesy of Place of the Governors Photo Archive, New Mexico History Museum (NMHM DCS), #015727.*

When the army in 1873 called for Navajos to join the military and become scouts, Mariano traveled the Checkerboard, encouraging enlistment of Navajo youth. He warned his people that if the Navajos did not want to be scouts, they would be forced to move out of the Checkerboard lands.[235]

Mariano's farsightedness in winning the favor of the military is the greatest legacy of the scouts, as it helped preserve a large portion of the Navajo homeland not included in the 1868 treaty.

The number of Navajos who enlisted and reenlisted as scouts, as well as the performance of the scouts in the field, won the support and admiration of many army officers. A friendly relationship between the army and the Navajos was important at this time because it was the military that had control over those Indians living outside reservation boundaries. The scouts, with the support of the military, were able to lessen the conflict between the Navajos and non-Indian ranchers and settlers.[236]

In time, there developed a level of respect and a positive relationship (for the most part) between the Navajo people and the United States military. As

Navajo Scouts During the Apache Wars

Navajo scouts Vicente and Germanita at Fort Wingate, 1880s. *Ben Wittick, courtesy of Place of the Governors Photo Archive, New Mexico History Museum (NMHM/DCS), #015712.*

former Navajo vice president Edward T. Begay stated, "What our leaders were able to accomplish at Hwéeldi [Fort Sumner, Bosque Redondo] was to give us a land, a home within the four sacred mountains, and a purpose as a people to live with our new partner, the United States, as a nation and a semi-independent entity within these borders."[237] This relationship, a feeling of partnership, was the genesis of Navajo fealty to the United States and the tradition of Navajo service in the military. Navajos enlisted in World War I, and as war clouds began to gather in 1940, the Navajo Nation Council on June 4 passed by unanimous vote a resolution titled a "Loyalty Pledge to the United States of America." This resolution was signed by Navajo council chairman Jacob C. Morgan, the son of Navajo scout Casamiro.

President Franklin Roosevelt responded to the Navajo Nation's action by noting, "I sincerely hope that it may never be necessary to call upon the Navajo Tribe to take up arms against a common enemy, but I shall always remember that it stood ready in these times of uncertainty."[238]

When war did come with the attack on Pearl Harbor by the Empire of Japan in 1941, many Navajos volunteered to serve. Historian Peter Iverson related the story that very soon after war was declared, hundreds of Navajo men came to the Navajo Nation's capital at Window Rock, Arizona, determined to enlist in the military.[239] The most famous of the Navajos who served were the Marine Corps' Code Talkers. Even before the start of World War II, the U.S. military was interested in the development of an unbreakable code to use in communication between troops in the field and to relay important information to and from officers in command. During World War I, indigenous languages were used to outwit the Germans. But it was Philip Johnson, a civil engineer in California, who proposed the use of a code using the Navajo language as a way of overcoming Japanese code breakers. Johnson, the son of a missionary, had spent much of his childhood on the Navajo Reservation and had learned the Navajo language from his Navajo playmates. In March 1942, Johnson was able to convince General Clayton Vogel, commanding officer of the Marine Corps' Pacific Fleet, that his idea would work.

In April 1942, 30 young Navajo men were enlisted at Wingate Boarding School and other Indian schools near the Navajo Reservation. After Marine Corps basic training, the remaining 29 Navajo marines devised a code using 413 words in addition to an alphabet based on the Navajo words. The code and the use of Navajo Code Talkers proved to be a success. By April 1943, 190 Code Talkers were in service, and by V-J Day in 1945, more than 400 Navajo men served as Code Talkers.[240] The Code Talkers in recent years have received much praise from historians and in popular culture.

NAVAJO SCOUTS DURING THE APACHE WARS

Navajo scouts, however, were not given the credit that they earned in accounts of the Apache Wars in New Mexico and Arizona. Most historians have given them minor notice, spending more time on Apache scouts. Lieutenant Charles B. Gatewood did much to devalue the role of Navajo scouts in his April 1894 article in the *Great Divide* titled "Campaigning Against Victorio in 1879," in which he said that "the few scouts and trailers in the service in New Mexico were enlisted from the Navajo and compared to the Apache Scouts of Arizona, belong to the coffee-cooling class and with few exceptions made serious objections to following a trail that was getting warm."[241] This quote unfortunately makes its way into almost every account of Navajo scouts. The record of Navajo scouts does not show them to be lazy or nonaggressive. What the record does show is that Navajos displayed all the military virtues and proved themselves to be loyal. There were only minor disciplinary incidents concerning Navajo scouts and certainly not the major mutiny of Apache scouts as at Cibecue. Regrettably, army officers who served with Navajo scouts such as Lieutenant Henry H. Wright and Captain Frank Bennett did not write a memoir of their service with Navajo scouts.

Young Navajos being sworn in as Marine Corps Code Talkers at Wingate Boarding School. *Courtesy of National Archives and Records, Washington, D.C.*

Navajo Code Talkers on duty in the Pacific during World War II. *Courtesy of National Archives and Records, Washington, D.C.*

Captain Henry H. Wright with other officers in the 1890s. Captain Wright is in the first row, third from left. *Courtesy of Wikimedia Commons.*

Navajo Scouts During the Apache Wars

The relationship between the military and the Navajo people has come under a degree of critical analysis recently by activist and writer Winona La Duke and Navajo historian Jennifer Nez Denetdale, who question the ongoing relationship of Indian people with the military in spite of a history of land appropriation, colonization, deculturalization and oppression of indigenous people by the military. La Duke also questions the militarization of the Navajo economy that had its beginning in the 1800s.[242] Historian Al Carroll, however, in his book *Medicine Bags and Dog Tags: American Indian Veterans from Colonial Times to the Second Iraq War*, stated that the military provided a means for cultural preservation, revival and defense in a way that few other Anglo-American institutions have been able to do.[243]

Navajo scouts have recently gained the attention of the military with the discovery by retired lieutenant colonel David C'de Baca that two Navajo women, Mexicana Chiquito and Muchacha, were enlisted as scouts by the Twentieth Regiment of the U.S. Infantry at Fort Wingate, New Mexico, in 1886. C'de Baca was working on a project for the Sandoval County Historical Society when he came across their names. Wishing to confirm his discovery, C'de Baca, with the help of New Mexico senator Tom Udall, was able to obtain the women's military records from the National Archives and Records Administration.[244] Once their service was authenticated, the

General Hugh Scott and old Navajo scouts reunion at Fort Wingate, 1900s. *Courtesy of G.E.E. Lindquist Collection, Buke Library, Columbia University, #864 box 51:741.*

United States Army Women's Museum of Fort Lee, Virginia, honored the women scouts at the Annual Veterans Summit held in Gallup, New Mexico, on October 12–13, 2016.[245]

Navajo scouts have for the most part been neglected in the popular literature of the West. There are many fictional accounts of Apache scouts, but few of Navajo scouts. An exception is New Mexico author Max Evans's portrayal of Navajo scouts in his romantic novel, *Faraway Blue*, about Buffalo Soldiers in New Mexico.[246] Film has continued this neglect. Although there are many westerns, from B grade to the very best, that portray Indian scouts, only John Ford's 1950 film *Rio Grande* features Navajo scouts. *Rio Grande* is a fictional account of an 1873 expedition into Mexico by the Fourth Cavalry Regiment under Colonel Ranald S. MacKenzie in pursuit of hostile Apaches. The film ends with a formation of Navajo scouts and cavalry troopers and the awarding of a citation to Navajo scout Son of Many Mules.[247]

The memory of the Navajo scouts is alive today in family stories about their ancestors in a display at the Navajo Nation Museum and in the "Fighting Scouts" mascot of Window Rock High School and the Navajo Scouts Hot Shot Wild-Lands Fire Team.

The scouts themselves left a legacy of leadership within their families, clans, communities and the Navajo Nation. Many returned from military service to serve their people as local headmen and peace officers and through serving as consultants to anthropologists helped to present the Navajo worldview to a wider audience. These returning veterans helped to guide the people through the difficult period in Navajo history from the return in 1868 to the beginning of the twentieth century, a time when the Navajos were able to develop a viable cultural and economic base. This foundation was able to resist and withstand the forces of colonialism and assimilation.[248]

Appendix

FAMOUS SCOUTS

JOSE CHAVEZ

Jose Chavez enlisted as a scout more times than any other Navajo during the period of the Apache Wars—more than fifteen times. His first enlistment was on December 1, 1876, at Fort Wingate, and he served with Second Lieutenant Henry Havilland Wright of the Ninth Cavalry. Both men were soon posted at Fort Bayard, New Mexico. They saw action in the Florida Mountains of New Mexico early in 1877, when Lieutenant Wright with six cavalry troopers and three Navajo scouts came upon an Apache camp. Wright, seeing that he was outnumbered, proposed talks with the Apaches. When talks failed, a bitter hand-to-hand fight broke out. Due to their courage, the Buffalo Soldiers and the Navajo scouts were able to fight their way out of the Apache camp and return to Fort Bayard without the loss of a single man. In this action, Jose Chavez was cited for bravery.

Chavez reenlisted in both June and December 1877, again serving with Lieutenant Wright of the Ninth. He enlisted again in 1878, this time at Ojo Caliente, New Mexico. The Buffalo Soldiers of the Ninth and the Navajo scouts during 1877 and 1878 were in action almost continually against Victorio and his band's resistance to being sent to San Carlos Reservation in Arizona. Chavez reenlisted in 1879 to serve with the Ninth.

Jose Chavez did not return to service until May 1886, when he joined the Sixth Cavalry at Fort Wingate to take part in the Geronimo campaign; at

Appendix

Left: Two Navajo scouts in 1906 army uniform at Fort Wingate, New Mexico. The scout on the right is probably Jeff King. *Simeon Schwemberger, courtesy of National Anthropological Archives, Washington, D.C., #NMNH-03266600.*

Right: Tombstone of scout Jose Chavez at the Santa Fe, New Mexico National Cemetery. *Courtesy of Marlane Taylor.*

this time, his age is listed as thirty-two. Jose Chavez was promoted to first sergeant and assigned to Company B under Lieutenant Charles Gatewood. Scout Jose Chavez enlisted in 1888, 1889 and 1890.[249]

In 1891, Jose Chavez, due to changes in War Department policy, was enlisted to a five-year term in Troop L of the Second Cavalry. He was a soldier until his death on June 14, 1898. His pension files show that he had two widows, Kid-Des-Pah and Ahe-Yi-Bah. First Sergeant Jose Chavez was first buried at the cemetery at Fort Wingate and then reinterred at the Santa Fe National Cemetery some years later.[250]

John Daw

John Daw was the last of the Navajo scouts, according to J. Lee Correll's story in the *Navajo Times* of June 24, 1965. Daw was born at Cottonwood

Pass near Newcomb in New Mexico soon after the Navajos returned from Fort Sumner. He died on June 15, 1965, near Cow Springs, Arizona.[251]

John Daw enlisted in the Second U.S. Cavalry, Company L, on May 7, 1891, for a five-year term of service. In 1890, the War Department began a policy of enlisting Indian soldiers into all Indian units for a term of five years. Although many of these units still served as scouts, they were now known as soldiers and received the same training as other recruits.

John Daw discussed his service and training during this period at an Indian Claims Commission meeting on January 1951: "I was given a uniform and taken in as a soldier. We went to a lot of training, target practices, and we were issued guns and ammunition and horses and took very extensive military training until we were highly trained as soldiers."

During his term of service, John was noted as an excellent soldier. He became his company's trumpeter and was promoted to corporal.

John Daw also served as a Navajo scout in 1886 during the Geronimo campaign. He enlisted, along with 150 others, at Fort Wingate, New Mexico. John remembered the march from Fort Wingate to the Apache country in Arizona. He said that three Navajo scouts were left behind at twenty-five-mile intervals in order to relay any messages back to Fort Wingate.

John was eighteen years old during the Geronimo campaign, and later in life, he told his daughter, Betty Lee, of his adventures. John, his family said, loved to tell war stories while riding his horse or driving a wagon. He had part of a finger missing and told the story that an Apache had shot it off. John summed up his Apache War experience in a story he told Betty: "And so we went to war and fought. Who our enemies were I do not know. We killed them and left them lying around. We piled up the guns and set fire to it and started to come back. We come [sic] back to Fort Wingate and we were all discharged as soon as we come [sic] back."[252]

Like many other scout veterans, John Daw became a law enforcement officer after his military service. In 1905, he was assigned to the newly established Western Navajo Agency in Tuba City, Arizona. For several years, his principal residence was at Red Lake Trading Post, about twenty miles from the agency. In addition to his job with the police, he operated a freight line, hauling supplies and goods to and from Flagstaff, Arizona.[253]

In 1923, the Richardsons, an Indian trading family, planned to establish a road to Rainbow Bridge and a tourist lodge and trading post in the area of Rainbow Bridge. Hubert and S.I. Richardson contacted John Daw at Red Lake, who told them that the only way to get to the area of the Rainbow Bridge was to take the "Old Ute War Trail." John told them that others have

Appendix

Navajo scout John Daw in later years, with granddaughter Louise Daw. *Courtesy of Cline Library, Northern Arizona University, Flagstaff, Arizona, NAU.516.117-5181.*

forgotten it, but he could take them over it. Happy to hear that there was a way to reach the bridge on a trail that could be developed for automobile travel, the Richardsons began construction in 1924. They hired John Daw as interpreter and to recruit Navajo laborers.

The establishment of a road became a matter of conflict between the Richardsons and John Wetherill, who was the first to open the Rainbow Bridge to tourists, guiding them over a difficult trail from his trading post at Kayenta, Arizona. The rivalry between the two trading families led to bitter discord between the Navajo communities of Red Valley and Kayenta. On several occasions, anti-road Navajos harassed the road builders with threats, telling them that they would be killed if they did not quit working. At one point, guns were drawn, and at another time, a melee of fistfights broke out. John Daw was able to end the conflict by confronting several armed and mounted Navajos, telling them if they wished to fight, fine, but his group had a road to build. He then said that they were fools to be drawn into a white man's fight, and if there was trouble out here, it would be Navajos who would go to jail and not whites. The situation calmed down, and by the next day, the Kayenta Navajos had ridden away without a word.[254] The Rainbow Trail and the Rainbow Lodge were completed without further incident.

As a member of the Navajo Mounted Patrol, Daw was noted as a tracker and, in 1937, attracted national attention when he was able to locate the body of a murdered prospector found near Kaibito, Arizona. A witness saw an Indian on a yellow horse leaving the scene of the murder. Thus, the case became known as the "Yellow Horse Murder." Because the shoes of the victim had been removed, Daw knew that no Navajo was involved, as they would not take personal items from a corpse. Daw soon found the killer, a Paiute, who surrendered once he knew that Daw was on the case. Daw's role in this case was reported in *True Detective Magazine* in 1939. The article stated that when the FBI wanted a tracker, it called for the old scout John Daw.[255]

In his later years, John Daw became a prominent medicine man and owned a trading post at Tonalea, Arizona.[256] During and after World War II, he performed healing ceremonies for veterans. In the 1950s, he testified before the Indian Claims Commission, retelling the stories his parents and grandparents had told him about the Long Walk and the return from Fort Sumner.[257]

John Daw, his family said, was always proud of his service as a Navajo scout, and when he dressed up, he always wore a string of beads around his neck, a blue bandana and his Indian Wars Metal.[258]

Jeff King (aka Hashka-zilth-e-yah)

Jeff King was born in about 1865 into the Kiiyaáanni clan for Bilaganna.[259] He may have gone to Fort Sumner as a child and returned with his family in 1868 to the old Fort Lyon site, now refitted and renamed Fort Wingate. Fort Wingate would play a major role in Jeff's life.

Jeff King's military record, from the National Archives in Washington, D.C., shows that he enlisted in Company L of the Second U.S. Cavalry, at Fort Wingate on May 3, 1891, and was discharged on August 2, 1894. He then reenlisted on July 23, 1898, and was discharged on July 22, 1908.[260]

In 1891, the U.S. military began a social experiment in which Indian men were enlisted into the army not with a six-month service as scouts but as regular soldiers serving five-year enlistments. Navajos enlisted at this time at Fort Wingate continued to serve in a scouting capacity but were governed under the new guidelines.[261]

During his term of enlistment, Jeff King rose to the rank of sergeant and participated in the June and July 1891 expedition to the Hopi village

Appendix

Old Navajo scout Jeff King. Most famous of all the scouts, he was the first Navajo to be buried at Arlington National Cemetery. *Courtesy of Navajo Nation Museum, Window Rock, Arizona.*

of Oraibi to place Hopi children in Keam's Canyon Boarding School.[262]

During his time in the cavalry, King did various jobs. He was a mail carrier, taking mail from Forts Wingate and Defiance to St. Johns, Arizona. He helped as a cook and in the post infirmary.[263] He saw more active service in 1897 when he and other Navajo scouts were called out to track the High Five Gang of train robbers. King and the other scouts found the robbers near Fence Lake, New Mexico. After a deadly shootout, the survivors were arrested.[264] Sergeant King is also credited in serving in the Pershing Expedition to capture Pancho Villa.[265] There are many stories of King's service as a scout during the Geronimo campaign of 1886. Few of the stories that Jeff told had to do with combat, however, because as his granddaughter remarked, "Traditional warriors would only share their experiences with other warriors and medicine people."[266]

Jeff King did say that when he was out scouting, the animals would warn him of the enemy's location. One time, Jeff said he rode close to the edge of a cliff when a black bear came in front of him and would not let him pass. When the bear moved at last, King looked over the edge and saw a lot of Apaches waiting in ambush. The bear had saved his life.[267]

After nearly thirty years of military service, Jeff King returned to the Navajo Nation, proud of his service as a scout to Generals Crook and Pershing.[268]

He returned to a peaceful life as a rancher and medicine man. Jeff, like many other scout veterans, became a leader in his community of Pinedale, New Mexico. Years after his service, he was elected to two terms as a delegate to the Navajo Tribal Council.[269] He made several trips to Washington, D.C., on behalf of the Navajo people. On January 10, 1917, Jeff King, Henry Chee Dodge and several other Navajos were photographed on the steps of the United States Capitol. In 1927, he went to Washington, D.C., with Agent S.F. Stacher and several other old scouts to meet with government officials.[270]

Jeff King became a very strong hataalii (singer) and a Yé ii dancer. He practiced the "Blessing Way," "The Enemy Way" and "Where the Two Who Came to Their Father." He was much in demand to do ceremonies for people, and during World War II, he performed protection ceremonies for Navajo soldiers, including the Code Talkers, going to war.[271]

Jeff King's knowledge of Navajo Chant Ways brought him to the attention of artist-ethnologist Maud Oaks, who in 1942 asked him to share the Navajo War Chant Way with her. Jeff agreed because he felt that few young men were willing to take the time to learn the complex songs and sand paintings needed to perform the "Where the Two Who Came to Their Father" chant way correctly—where it is performed as a protection for the Navajo warrior going off to war and to provide comfort to those left behind. The song is performed to protect the souls of the warrior and to help to keep them in Hozho, or harmony.

Maud Oaks worked with Jeff King in 1942 and 1943 and then published what she had learned from Jeff King. Her book became well known for its accuracy and the beauty of the sand paintings.

Fort Wingate celebrated its centennial in 1960, and Jeff King was the grand marshal of the event. He was honored by this statement in the event program: "Wisdom, memories, pride, devotion to those things valuable, the warmth and dignity that give true stature, these make the spirit and the man that is Jeff King....The warmth and dignity of the man and of the Indian people. This is the spirit of Jeff King—and the spirit of the past one hundred years we now celebrate."[272]

For the occasion, a horseshoe-shaped monument, constructed from some of the building stones of the old fort, was blessed by Jeff King. He also blessed the new buildings of Wingate High School.[273]

During the year 1960, Jeff King made a visit to New York City and, as part of a delegation, met with high-ranking military leaders in Washington, D.C. During the tour, he visited Arlington National Cemetery, and at that time, he requested to be interred there. When Sergeant Jeff King passed on in 1965, he was laid to rest at Arlington with full honors, including a horse-drawn caisson, an honor usually reserved for officers.[274]

Tom Torlino

Tom Torlino is best known for the before and after pictures of a young Navajo man taken at the Carlisle Indian Industrial School in the 1880s. He is the example of the government's policy to assimilate the American Indian. He is depicted as a victim of that policy. Tom entered Carlisle on

Appendix

Tom Torlino's before and after images taken at Carlisle Indian School. *John N. Choate, 1882–85, courtesy of Wikimedia Commons.*

October 21, 1882, and left the school on August 28, 1886, a period of about four years.

Carlisle was established in 1879 by Civil War and Indian Wars veteran Richard Henry Pratt. The educational goal of Carlisle was the ultimate and complete civilization of the Indian.[275] At that time, American values were defined as Christian and Euro-American. The goal was to be accomplished by replacing native religion, customs, culture, skills, games and loyalties with those of America. Students lived in a military-like environment and each morning saluted the Stars and Stripes. They played baseball and football and went to church and Sunday school. Students were not to use their language, and the enrollment was made up of students from many different native nations. This mixture was planned to break down tribal identity. A key factor in the Carlisle program was the Outing System, by which Indian youth were placed with white tradesmen and farmers to learn useful skills and to live like the white man.[276] Tom Torlino's student record at Carlisle notes that he was enrolled in the Outing System first in 1883 with Hugh Thomas as his mentor and in 1886 with C.M. Siever. Both men were probably farmers, and Tom was expected to help with the farm work.[277]

Tom left Carlisle in 1886 and returned home to Coyote Canyon, New Mexico. Following a period of readjusting to Navajo life, Tom became a rancher and medicine man.[278]

Appendix

Old Navajo scout Tom Torlino. He attended Carlisle Indian School and after his service became a noted rancher and community leader. *Courtesy of Navajo Nation Museum, Window Rock, Arizona.*

The skills he learned at Carlisle proved useful when he was asked by his uncle, Chief Manuelito, to write a letter to the U.S. Army Corps of Engineers requesting help in building a water system at Coyote Canyon. Lieutenant Brown was sent to work with the Navajos on this project. He was also enlisting Navajos for military service. It was at this time that Tom Torlino enlisted in Company L of the Navajo Indian scouts at Fort Wingate.[279] After his service, he returned home and became known for raising fine racing horses.[280]

Francisco

Francisco was born sometime in the 1850s and became a local headman. During the Navajo War, he was captured by New Mexicans and became the slave of Antonio Manzanares of Abiquiu in northern New Mexico.

By 1868 he was at Fort Sumner and was involved in the treaty negotiations and was one of the leaders who signed the Navajo Treaty on June 1, 1868.

Francisco returned to the Navajo Nation with the other Navajos in 1868 and settled with his relatives and worked to restore the Navajo Nation. In 1885, at the age of thirty, he enlisted as a Navajo Indian scout at Fort Wingate and served in the Geronimo campaign. In 1922, due to the efforts of Eastern Navajo agent S.F. Stacher, Francisco was granted a pension.

Along with other Indian scout veterans, he was awarded a Federal Indian Wars Campaign medal for valor and courage during the Apache Wars. Francisco died in 1942.[281]

JESUS ARVISO

Jesus Arviso was born in Mexico and at a very early age was captured by Apache raiders, who in about 1850 traded him to a Navajo named B'ee Lizhine (Black Shirt) for a pony. Jesus grew up with the Navajos and was called Tl'aii (Cly) because he was left handed. He soon learned the Navajo language but retained his native Spanish. Arviso's bilingual skills shaped the rest of his life.

During General Canby's 1860–61 campaign against the Navajos, Jesus's Navajo family sent him to seek peace with the Americans. He rode into the camp of Captain Lafayette McLaws (later a Confederate general) holding a white sheepskin as a flag of truce. McLaws explained to Jesus that he was not authorized to make peace, but McLaws was so impressed with young Arviso that he employed him as a guide and interpreter.

Old Navajo scout Jesus Arviso. As a child, he was sold by the Apaches to the Navajos and became their interpreter at Fort Sumner. *Courtesy of Navajo Nation Museum, Window Rock, Arizona.*

When the Navajo War began in 1863, Arviso was an interpreter at Fort Wingate and brought in Navajo leaders to discuss General Carleton's terms for surrender and removal to Fort Sumner. Most of these men refused to be relocated voluntarily, and the Navajo campaign began. In 1865, Jesus Arviso was at Fort Sumner as an interpreter. During his time there, he married a Navajo woman named Yohazbaá. He also made many trips back to the Navajo country with other Red Shirts to encourage Navajos to come out of hiding and go to Fort Sumner.

During the treaty negotiations in May 1868, he was the official interpreter going from Navajo to Spanish. Because Arviso spoke no English, the Spanish-to-English transmission was carried out by another interpreter.

Appendix

When the Navajos were allowed to return home after the treaty was signed on June 1, 1868, Arviso returned home with them. He began ranching on his wife's family area east of Tohatchi, New Mexico, and took an additional wife and had a large family. In 1872, he was working at the Fort Defiance Agency and was with Agent James H. Miller and Thomas V. Keam when they were attacked by Utes during an expedition to the San Juan River Valley to locate a new site for an agency. Agent Miller was killed in the attack, and Keam and Arviso were lucky to escape.

In 1874, Arviso accompanied Navajo agent William F.M. Arny and a delegation of Navajo leaders—including Manuelito; his wife, Juanita; and Mariano—to Washington, D.C. By 1875, the Navajo leadership had grown tired of Agent Arny and asked that he be removed. When the government ignored this request, the Navajos took over the agency buildings at Fort Defiance. In response to this action, Arny was removed.

In the 1880s and early 1890s, Arviso served as interpreter for the Navajo scouts at Fort Wingate. A major duty was to serve as Navajo-Spanish interpreter at military trials.

In the 1920s, Jesus Arviso, through Superintendent Samuel F. Stacher at the Crownpoint Agency, applied for a scout's pension, but in spite of Stacher's support—even requesting a special act of Congress—Arviso's pension was denied because he was never enlisted as a scout and served as a civilian employee.

Jesus Arviso died in 1932 and is buried at Cubero, New Mexico.[282]

Notes

Chapter 1

1. Dunbar-Ortiz, *Indigenous Peoples' History*, 148.
2. Hendricks and Wilson, *Navajos in 1705*, 3–4.
3. Collman, "Navajo Scouts, 1873–1895," 9–11.
4. Hauptman, "Cadet David Moniac," 342.
5. Hauptman, *Between Two Fires*, 17–23.
6. Ibid., 161–70.
7. Largent, "Iroquois Chief and Union Officer," 54.
8. Ibid., 58.
9. Hauptman, *Iroquois in the Civil War*, 58.
10. Hardoff, *Cheyenne Memories*, 125.
11. Hutton and Ball, *Soldiers West*, 89.
12. Ibid., 93.
13. Thompson, *Desert Tiger*, 4–5.
14. Stout, *Apache Lightning*, 56–59.
15. Kenner, *Buffalo Soldiers and Officers*, 9.
16. Viola, *Warriors in Uniform*, 43.
17. Dunlay, *Wolves for the Blue Soldiers*, 56.
18. Tyler, *History of Indian Policy*, 73.
19. Dunlay, *Wolves for the Blue Soldiers*, 207.
20. Ibid., 24.
21. Ibid., 192.
22. Hutton and Ball, *Soldiers West*, 261.
23. Viola, *Warriors in Uniform*, 58–61.

24. Mason, "Use of Indian Scouts," 17.
25. Ibid., 34.
26. Britten, *American Indians in World War I*, 26.
27. Dunlay, *Wolves for the Blue Soldiers*, 208.
28. Ibid., 191.
29. Smitts, "Indian Scouts and Indian Allies," 329.
30. Ibid., 330–31.
31. Dunlay, *Wolves for the Blue Soldiers*, 197.
32. Collman, "Navajo Scouts, 1873–1895," 57.
33. Arizona Civil War Council website.
34. Malone, "On the Trail of Geronimo," 43, 44.
35. Dunlay, *Wolves for the Blue Solders*, 80.
36. Smitts, "Indian Scouts and Indian Allies," 336.
37. Dunlay, *Wolves for the Blue Solders*, 80.
38. Smitts, "Indian Scouts and Indian Allies," 332.

Chapter 2

39. Iverson, *Diné*, 30, 34.
40. Correll, *Through White Men's Eyes*, 171–75.
41. Jones, "Origins of the Navajo Police," 226.
42. Ibid., 227.
43. Ibid., 229.
44. Moore, *Chiefs, Agents and Soldiers*, 187.
45. Howard, *My Life and Experiences*, 181.
46. Jones, "Origins of the Navajo Police," 230.
47. Bender, *New Hope for the Indians*, 81.
48. Moore, *Chiefs, Agents and Soldiers*, 99, 100.
49. Jones, "Origins of the Navajo Police," 230–31.
50. Underhill, *Here Come the Navajo!*, 204.
51. Jones, "Origins of the Navajo Police," 232–34.

Chapter 3

52. Heyman, *Prudent Soldier*, 131.
53. Apache, "Navajo War: Interview with Tom Ration," 19–25.
54. Collman, "Navajo Scouts, 1873–1895," 18–21.
55. Ibid., 54.
56. *History of Fort Wingate Depot*, 63.
57. Denetdale, *Reclaiming Diné History*, 170–72.

Chapter 4

58. Goodwin, *Western Apache Raiding and Warfare*, 12, 13.
59. Ibid., 38, 39.
60. Davisson and Perry, *Dispatches from the Fort Apache Scouts*, 60.
61. Moore, *Chiefs, Agents and Soldiers*, 198.
62. Goodwin, *Western Apache Raiding and Warfare*, 52, 53.
63. Aleshire, *Warrior Woman*, 82.
64. Cermony, *Life Among the Apaches*, 308.
65. Colyer, *Peace with the Apaches*, 5.
66. Ball, *INDEH*, 200.
67. Cermony, *Life Among the Apaches*, 308.
68. Shapard, *Chief Loco*, 148.
69. Roessel, *Navajo Stories of the Long Walk Period*, 153.

Chapter 5

70. Watt, *Apache Tactics*, 15.
71. Goodwin, *Western Apache*, 16, 17.
72. Watt, *Apache Tactics*, 18.
73. Ibid., 20.
74. Hutton, *Apache Wars*, 228.
75. Greene, *Indian War Veterans Memories*, 74.
76. Watt, *Apache Tactics*, 14–16.
77. Ibid., 44.
78. *Fort Hauchuca Illustrated* 7, "Apache Scouts," 16.
79. Hutton and Ball, *Soldiers West*, 305.
80. Thrapp, *Al Sieber, Chief of Scouts*, 89.

Chapter 6

81. Hehren, "Scouting for Mescaleros," 171–90.
82. Collman, "Navajo Scouts, 1873–1895," 23.
83. Hehren, "Scouting for Mescaleros," 175.
84. Michno, *Encyclopedia of Indian Wars*, 285; Carriker and McFadden, "Thompson McFadden's Diary," 198–232.
85. Carriker and McFadden, "Thompson McFadden's Diary," 213–14.
86. Moore, *Chiefs, Agents and Soldiers*, 146.
87. Nichols, *Lincoln and the Indians*, 154.
88. Utley and Washburn, *American Heritage History*, 193.

89. Watt, "Horses Worn to Mere Shadows," 198.
90. Utley, "Victorio's War," 21–22.
91. Collman, "Navajo Scouts, 1873–1895," 2, 4.
92. Leckie, *Buffalo Soldiers*, 113, 176–77.
93. Collman, "Navajo Scouts, 1873–1895," 25.
94. Leckie, *Buffalo Soldiers*, 178–79.
95. Hutton, *Apache Wars*, 244.
96. Gott, *In Search of an Elusive Enemy*, 14–17.
97. Collman, "Navajo Scouts, 1873–1895," 28, 29.
98. Ibid., 31.
99. Chamberlain, *Victorio Apache Warrior and Chief*, 155.
100. Moore, *Chiefs, Agents and Soldiers*, 176.
101. Hutton, *Apache Wars*, 229.
102. Graves, *Thomas Varker Keam*, 86.
103. Taylor, *Looking for Dan*, 10–12.
104. McNitt, *Indian Traders*, 137.
105. Taylor, *Looking for Dan*, 12.
106. Graves, *Thomas Varker Keam*, 85, 86.
107. Collman, "Navajo Scouts, 1873–1895," 51, 52; Moore, *Chiefs, Agents and Soldiers*, 176–77.
108. Graves, *Thomas Varker Keam*, 88, 89.

Chapter 7

109. Collman, "Navajo Scouts, 1873–1895," 32; Hutton, *Apache Wars*, 229.
110. Chamberlin, *Victorio Apache Chief*, 156–58; Moore, *Chiefs, Agents and Soldiers*, 206; Hutton, *Apache Wars*, 230–31; Thrapp, *Dan Victorio and the Mimbres Apaches*, 207–12.
111. Terrell, *Apache Chronicle*, 336–39.
112. Thrapp, *Dan Victorio and the Mimbres Apaches*, 220–51.
113. Wellman, *Death in the Desert*, 165.
114. Collman, "Navajo Scouts, 1873–1895," 37.
115. Stout, *Apache Lightning*, 92–100; Chamberlain, *Victorio Apache Chief*, 170–71.
116. Bower, "Massacre in Las Animas Canyon."
117. Stout, *Apache Lightning*, 92–100.
118. Bower, "Massacre in Las Animas Canyon."
119. Watt, "Horses Worn to Mere Shadows," 32.
120. Kenner, *Buffalo Soldiers and Officers*, 193.
121. Bower, "Massacre in Las Animas Canyon."

122. Terrell, *Apache Chronicle*, 338.
123. Collman, "Navajo Scouts, 1873–1895," 38.
124. Billington, *New Mexico's Buffalo Soldiers*, 88, 89.
125. Aleshire, *Reaping the Whirlwind*, 70.
126. Gott, *In Search of an Elusive Enemy*, 20; Hutton, *Apache Wars*, 236–37.
127. Tracking Nana, "Ambush in Gavilan Canyon," 7; Thrapp, *Dan Victorio and the Mimbres Apaches*, 195.
128. Collman, "Navajo Scouts, 1873–1895," 38, 39.
129. Thrapp, *Dan Victorio and the Mimbres Apaches*, 250.
130. *Arizona Citizen*, February 6, 1880.
131. Hutton, *Apache Wars*, 239.
132. *Arizona Citizen*, February 6, 1880.
133. Collman, "Navajo Scouts, 1873–1895," 42.
134. Hutton, *Apache Wars*, 240–42.
135. Collman, "Navajo Scouts, 1873–1895," 42; Thrapp, *Dan Victorio and the Mimbres Apaches*, 271–72.
136. Utley, "Victorio's War," 27, 28; Terrell, *Apache Chronicle*, 340.
137. Hutton, *Apache Wars*, 241.
138. Terrell, *Apache Chronicle*, 343.

Chapter 8

139. Hutton, *Apache Wars*, 261.
140. Watt, *Apache Tactics*, 17.
141. Lekson, "Nana's Raid," 32.
142. Bibo, "Ballad of Placida Romero," 292.
143. Tracking Nana, "Ambush in Gavilan Canyon," 25.
144. Bibo, "Ballad of Placida Romero," 295.
145. Lekson, "Nana's Raid," 27.
146. Tracking Nana, "Ambush in Gavilan Canyon," 41–45; Lekson, "Nana's Raid," 28–32.

Chapter 9

147. Wellman, *Indian Wars of the West*, 421.
148. Geronimo, *Geronimo*, 144.
149. Hutton, *Apache Wars*, 223.
150. Collins, *Apache Nightmare*, 30, 31, 230.
151. Shapard, *Chief Loco*, 144.

152. Ibid., 150.
153. Hutton, *Apache Wars*, 294.
154. *Arizona Sentinel*, "General Crook to Enlist 200 Navajo Indian Scouts."
155. Collman, "Navajo Scouts, 1873–1895," 50.
156. Ibid., 92.
157. Malone, "On the Trail of Geronimo," 41–47.
158. Utley and Washburn, *American Heritage History*, 284.
159. Cozzens, *Eyewitnesses to the Indian Wars*, 437.
160. Thrapp, *Juh*, 5.
161. Faulk, *Geronimo Campaign*, 71.
162. Collman, "Navajo Scouts, 1873–1895," 54.
163. *Fort Hauchuca Illustrated*, 55, 56; Britton, *Truth About Geronimo*, 196.
164. Collman, "Navajo Scouts, 1873–1895," 54, 56.
165. *Las Vegas Gazette*, January 8, 1886.
166. *Clifton Clarion*, August 4, 1886.
167. Collman, "Navajo Scouts, 1873–1895," 55.
168. Ibid., 56.
169. National Archives and Records Administration, Records of the Judge Advocate General Court-Martial Case Files, 1809–1894, RG 153, entry 15A.
170. Hutton, *Apache Wars*, 354.
171. Utley and Washburn, *American Heritage History*, 286–89.
172. Mason, "Use of Indian Scouts," 331.
173. *Weekly Commercial Herald*, June 4, 1886.
174. Brunt, "Historian: 2 Navajo Women"; see also Plante letter to Udall, May 24, 2016, Collection of Martin Link, Gallup, New Mexico.
175. *Silverbelt*, June 26, 1886.
176. Collman, "Navajo Scouts, 1873–1895," 68.
177. *Black Range*, August 18, 1886.
178. Collman, "Navajo Scouts, 1873–1895," 61.
179. Kraft, *Gatewood and Geronimo*, 116, 130.
180. Brown, *Bury My Heart at Wounded Knee*, 411.
181. Collman, "Navajo Scouts, 1873–1895," 61.
182. Ibid.
183. Ibid., 65.
184. Ball, *INDEH*, 106, 107.
185. Geronimo, *Geronimo*, 152.
186. *Arizona Citizen Weekly*, September 4, 1886; Ball, *INDEH*, 114.
187. Collman, "Navajo Scouts, 1873–1895," 61.

Chapter 10

188. Mitchell, *Navajo Blessingway Singer*, 104.
189. Collman, "Navajo Scouts, 1873–1895," 76, 77.
190. Ibid., 78.
191. Cuch, *History of Utah's American Indians*, 251.
192. Kempes-Poling, *Ladies of the Canyons*, 156–57.
193. *Holbrook News*, March 26, 1915.
194. Dunlay, *Wolves for the Blue Soldiers*, 35.
195. Tietjen, "Encounter with the Frontier," 57; Melzer and Taylor, *Tragic Trails and Enchanted Journeys*, 39–41.
196. Tietjen, "Encounter with the Frontier," 57.
197. Cousins and Cousins, *Tales from Wide Ruins*, 17–19.
198. *Albuquerque Daily Citizen*, June 26, 1900.
199. *Tombstone Epitaph*, May 29, 1892.
200. Waters, *Book of the Hopi*, 309–10.
201. Pershing, *My Life Before the World War*, 64.
202. Lahti, *Cultural Construction of Empire*, 113.
203. Baldwin, *Memoirs of the Late Major General*, 168; *Black Range*, August 18, 1886.

Chapter 11

204. Sixty-Fourth Congress, December 28, 1925, http://loc.gov.
205. C.R. Frank to S.F. Stacher, December 28, 1925, Navajo Nation Library-Archives.
206. S.F. Stacher to Commissioner of Pensions, July 10, 1925, U.S. National Archives and Records.
207. Stacher, "Recollections," 120.
208. Several letters to Stacher from Indian traders, Trader File, Navajo Nation Library-Archives.
209. S.F. Stacher File, Navajo Nation Library-Archives.
210. Ibid.
211. Tietjen, *Ramah*, 152.
212. Denetdale, *Reclaiming Diné History*, 170–71.
213. Link, *Navajo*, 28–29; Boelter, "Old Navajo Scouts."

Chapter 12

214. Collman, "Navajo Scouts, 1873–1895," 95.
215. Geronimo, *Geronimo*, 129.

216. Denetdale, *Reclaiming Diné History*, 170–72.
217. Collman, "Navajo Scouts, 1873–1895," 96–98.

Chapter 13

218. Some accounts say that one twin was born to White Shell Woman, the sister of Changing Woman.
219. Kluckholm and Leighton, *The Navajo*, 180–83; Zolbrod, *Diné Bahané*, 191–98.
220. Iverson, *Diné*, 11.
221. Ibid., 12.
222. Roessel, *Navajo Stories of the Long Walk Period*, xi.
223. Carroll, *Medicine Bags and Dog Tags*, 208–9.
224. Denetdale, *Reclaiming Diné History*, 170.
225. Roessel, *Long Walk*, x.
226. Heyman, *Prudent Soldier*, 114–25.
227. Collman, "Navajo Scouts, 1873–1895," 103.
228. Volkert, "Oral Navajo History," 1, 5.
229. Moore, *Chiefs, Agents and Soldiers*, 252.
230. Lyon, "American and Other Aliens," 152–54.

Chapter 14

231. *The Independent*, June 6, 2018, 4.
232. Kelley and Francis, "Few Improvements," 73–101.
233. Ibid.
234. Ibid., 88.
235. Collman, "Navajo Scouts, 1873–1895," 54.
236. Denetdale, "Securing Navajo National Boundaries," 137.
237. Iverson, *Diné*, 37.
238. Ibid., 179.
239. Ibid., 182.
240. Riseman, "Regardless of History?," 48–73.
241. Cozzens, *Eyewitnesses to the Indian Wars*, 214.
242. LaDuke and Cruz, *Militarization of Indian Country*, 27; Denetdale, "Securing Navajo National Boundaries," 141.
243. Carroll, *Medicine Bags and Dog Tags*, 223.
244. Brunt, "Historian: 2 Navajo Women."
245. Second Annual Veterans Summit in Gallup, New Mexico, October 12–13, 2016.

246. Evans, *Faraway Blue*.
247. Wikipedia, "*Rio Grande* (film)."
248. Iverson, *Diné*, 70.

Appendix

249. National Archives and Records, RG 94, enlistment papers, Indian scouts, 1866–1914.
250. Find a Grave, "Jose Chavez."
251. Correll, "John Daw."
252. Banks, "John Daw," 17.
253. Kunitz, *Drinking, Conduct Disorder and Social Change*, 31.
254. Richardson, *Navajo Trader*, 49–57.
255. Banks, "John Daw," 17.
256. Kelley and Francis, *Navajoland Trading Post Encyclopedia*.
257. Correll, "John Daw."
258. Banks, "John Daw," 17.
259. Manolescu, "Leading the Way," 2.
260. National Archives and Records, RG 94, enlistment papers, Indian scouts.
261. Collman, "Navajo Scouts, 1873–1895," 78–80.
262. National Archives and Records, RG 94, enlistment papers, Indian scouts.
263. Manolescu, "Leading the Way," 2–5.
264. Robinson, *El Malpais*, 100.
265. *Historical Program Fort Wingate Centennial*, 2.
266. Manolescu, "Leading the Way," 2–5.
267. Ibid.
268. Ibid.
269. Ibid., 5.
270. Ibid., 2–23; *Fort Wingate Centennial*, 4.
271. Manolescu, *Leading the Way*, 6–7.
272. *Fort Wingate Centennial*, 2.
273. *Independent*, August 29, 1960.
274. Manolescu, "Leading the Way," 31; *Navajo Times*, January 22, 2009.
275. DeJong, *Promises of the Past*, 109.
276. Ibid., 109–10.
277. Carlisle Indian School Digital Resource Center website.
278. Cindy Yurth, "Manuelito's Legacy."

279. Collman, "Navajo Scouts, 1873–1895," 80.
280. Ibid.
281. Harrison Lapahie; Collman, *Navajo Scouts*, 111.
282. Michaelis, *Navajo Treaty of 1868*, 63, 64.

Bibliography

Archives and Photograph Collections

Arizona State University Library, Hayden Labriola.
Center for Southwest Research, University of New Mexico.
Columbia University Library, G.E.E. Lindquist Native American Photo Collection.
Library of Congress, Washington, D.C.
National Archives and Records, Old Military Records, Washington, D.C.
Navajo Nation Library. Navajo Land Claims Papers. J. Lee Correll Collection, Old Scout, Window Rock, Arizona.

General Files

Northern Arizona University, Cline Library.
Place of the Governors Photo Archives, Santa Fe, New Mexico.
Pritzker Military Museum and Library.
Smithsonian National Museum of Natural History, National Anthropological Archives.
Wikimedia Commons Images.
Yale University Library, Beinecke Rare Books and Manuscripts Library.

Book, Booklets and Pamphlets

Aleshire, Peter. *Reaping the Whirlwind: The Apache Wars.* New York: Facts on File, 1998.

Bibliography

———. *Warrior Woman: The Story of Lozen, Apache Warrior and Shaman*. New York: St. Martins Press, 2001.

Altshuler, Constance Wynn. *Cavalry Yellow and Infantry Blue: Army Officers in Arizona between 1851 and 1886*. Tucson: Arizona Historical Society, 1991.

Bailey, Garrick, and Roberta Glenn Baily. *A History of the Navajos: The Reservation Years*. Santa Fe, NM: School of American Research Press, 1986.

Baldwin, Alice Blackwood. *Memoirs of the Late Major General Frank D. Baldwin*. Los Angeles: Wetzel Publishing Company, 1929.

Ball, Eve. *INDEH: An Apache Odyssey*. Norman: University of Oklahoma Press, 1980.

———. *In the Days of Victorio*. Tucson: University of Arizona Press, 2003.

Bender, Norman J. *New Hope for the Indians: The Grant Peace Policy and the Navajos in the 1870s*. Albuquerque: University of New Mexico Press, 1989.

Billington, Lee M. *New Mexico's Buffalo Soldiers, 1866–1900*. Niwot: University Press of Colorado, 1991.

Bourke, John G. *An Apache Campaign in the Sierra Madre*. N.p.: Pyrrhus Press. First published Charles Scribner's Sons, 1958. Digital kindle edition.

———. *On the Border with Crook*. Lincoln: University of Nebraska Press, 1971.

Britten, Thomas A. *American Indians in World War I, at Home and at War*. Albuquerque: University of New Mexico Press, 1997.

Britton, Davis. *The Truth About Geronimo*. New Haven, CT: Yale University Press, 1963. First printing, 1929.

Broder, Patricia Janis. *Shadows on Glass: The Indian World of Ben Wittick*. Savage, MD: Rowman and Littlefield, 1990.

Brown, Dee. *Bury My Heart at Wounded Knee*. New York: Holt, Rinehart & Winston, 1970.

Carroll, Al. *Medicine Bags and Dog Tags: American Indian Veterans from Colonial Times to the Second Iraq War*. Lincoln: University of Nebraska Press, 2008.

Cermony, John C. *Life Among the Apaches, 1850–1868*. Glorieta, NM: Rio Grande Press, 1969. First printing, 1868.

Chamberlain, Kathleen P. *Victorio Apache Warrior and Chief*. Norman: University of Oklahoma Press, 2007.

Collins, Charles. *Apache Nightmare: The Battle at Cibecue Creek*. Norman: University of Oklahoma Press, 1999.

Colyer, Vincent. *Peace with the Apaches of New Mexico and Arizona*. Washington, D.C.: Government Printing Office, 1872.

Cook, James H. *Fifty Years on the Frontier as Cowboy, Hunter, Guide, Scout and Ranchman*. Norman: University of Oklahoma Press, 1980. First printing, Yale University Press, 1923.

Correll, Lee J. *Through White Men's Eyes: A Contribution to Navajo History*. Window Rock, AZ: Navajo Heritage Center, 1976.

Bibliography

Cousins, Jean, and Bill Cousins. *Tales from Wide Ruins*. Edited by Mary Tate Engles. Lubbock: Texas University Press, 1996.

Cozzens, Peter. *The Earth Is Weeping: The Epic Story of the Indian Wars for the American West*. New York: Alfred A. Knopf, 2016.

Cozzens, Peter, ed. *Eyewitnesses to the Indian Wars, 1865–1890: The Struggle for Apacheria*. Mechanicsburg, PA: Stackpole Books, 2001.

Cuch, Forrest, ed. *A History of Utah's American Indians*. Salt Lake City: Utah Division of Indian Affairs and Division of State History, 2000.

Davisson, Lori, and Edgar Perry. *Dispatches from the Fort Apache Scouts*. Tucson: University of Arizona Press, 2016.

Debo, Angie. *Geronimo: The Man, the Time, His Place*. Norman: University of Oklahoma Press, 1976.

DeJong, David H. *Promises of the Past: A History of Indian Education*. Golden, CO: North American Press, 1993.

Denetdale, Jennifer Nez. *Reclaiming Diné History: The Legacies of Navajo Chief Manuelito and Juanita*. Tucson: University of Arizona Press, 2007.

Dunbar-Ortiz, Roxanne. *An Indigenous Peoples' History of the United States*. Boston: Beacon Press, 2014.

Dunlay, Thomas W. *Wolves for the Blue Soldiers: Indian Scouts and Auxiliaries with the United States Army, 1860–90*. Lincoln: University of Nebraska Press, 1982.

Evans, Max. *Faraway Blue*. Albuquerque: University of New Mexico Press, 1996.

Faris, James C. *Navajo and Photography: A Critical History of the Representation of an American People*. Albuquerque: University of New Mexico Press, 1996.

Faulk, Odie B. *The Geronimo Campaign*. New York: Oxford University Press, 1969.

Fixico, Donald. "Ethics and Responsibilities in Writing American Indian History." In *Major Problems in American Indian History*. Edited by Albert L. Hurtado and Peter Iverson. New York: Houghton Mifflin Company, 2001.

Frazer, Robert W. *Forts and Supplies: The Role of the Army in the Economy of the Southwest, 1846–1861*. Albuquerque: University of New Mexico Press, 1983.

Frink, Maurice, with Casey Barthelmess. *Photographer on an Army Mule*. Norman: University of Oklahoma Press, 1965.

Geronimo. *Geronimo: His Own Story*. Edited by S.M. Barrett. New York: Ballantine Books, 1971.

Goodwin, Grenville. *Western Apache Raiding and Warfare*. Edited by Keith H. Basso. Tucson: University of Arizona Press, 1971.

Goossen, Irvy W. *Diné Bizaad: Speak, Read, Write Navajo*. Flagstaff, AZ: Salina Bookshelf, 1995.

Gott, Kendall D. *In Search of an Elusive Enemy: The Victorio Campaign*. Fort Leavenworth, KS: Combat Studies Institute Press, 2002.

Graves, Laura. *Thomas Varker Keam, Indian Trader.* Norman: University of Oklahoma Press, 1998.

Greenberg, Henry, and Georgia Greenberg. *Power of a Navajo Carl Gorman: The Man and His Life.* Santa Fe, NM: Clear Light Publishers, 1966.

Greene, Jerome A. *Indian War Veterans Memories of Army Life and Campaigns in the West, 1864–1898.* New York: Savas Beatie, 2007.

Hammond-Hazen, Susan. *Timelines of Native American History.* New York: Perigee Book, 1997.

Hardoff, Richard G. *Cheyenne Memories of the Custer Fight.* Lincoln: University of Nebraska Press, 1995.

Hauptman, Laurence M. *Between Two Fires: American Indians in the Civil War.* New York: Free Press Paperbacks, 1996.

———. *The Iroquois in the Civil War: From Battlefield to Reservation.* Syracuse, NY: University Press, 1993.

Hendricks, Rick, and John P. Wilson. *The Navajos in 1705.* Albuquerque: University of New Mexico Press, 1996.

Heyman, Max L., Jr. *Prudent Soldier: A Biography of Major General E.R.S. Canby, 1917–1873.* Glendale, CA: Arthur H. Clark Company, 1959.

Historical Program Fort Wingate Centennial, August 25, 26, 27, 28, 1960. Fort Wingate Ordinance Depot. Gallup, NM: U.S. Department of the Army.

History of Fort Wingate Depot, Forts Fauntleroy and Lyon. U.S. Army DAR COM, 1960.

Howard, Oliver O. *My Life and Experiences Among Our Hostile Indians.* Hartford, CT: A.T. Worthington, 1907. Republished, New York: De Capo Press, 1972.

Hoxie, Frederick E., ed. *Indians in American History: An Introduction.* D'Arcy McNickle Center for the History of the American Indian. Arlington Heights, IL: Harlan Davidson Inc., 1988.

Hutton, Paul Andrew. *The Apache Wars.* New York: Crown Publishing, 2016.

Hutton, Paul Andrew, and Durwood Ball. *Soldiers West: Biographies from the Military Frontier.* Norman: University of Oklahoma Press, 2009.

Iverson, Peter. *Diné A History of the Navajos.* Albuquerque: University of New Mexico Press, 2002.

———. *The Navajo Nation.* Albuquerque: University of New Mexico Press, 1981.

Johnson, Broderick H., ed. *Stories of Navajo Life and Culture.* Tsaile, AZ: Navajo Community College Press, 1977.

Kelley, Klara, and Harris Francis. *Navajoland Trading Post Encyclopedia.* Window Rock, AZ: Navajo Nation Heritage and Historic Preservation Department, 2018.

Kempes-Poling, Lesley. *Ladies of the Canyons: A League of Extraordinary Women and Their Adventures in the American Southwest.* Tucson: University of Arizona Press, 2015.

Bibliography

Kenner, Charles L. *Buffalo Soldiers and Officers of the Ninth Cavalry, 18671898: Black and White Together.* Norman: University of Oklahoma Press, 1999.

King, James T. *War Eagle: A Life of General Eugene A. Carr.* Lincoln: University of Nebraska Press, 1963.

Kluckholm, Clyde, and Dorothea Leighton. *The Navajo.* N.p.: Anchor Books, 1962.

Kraft, Louis. *Gatewood and Geronimo.* Albuquerque: University of New Mexico Press, 2000.

Kunitz, Stephen. *Drinking, Conduct Disorder and Social Change: Navajo Experiences.* New York: Oxford University Press, 2000.

LaDuke, Winona, and Sean Aaron Cruz. *The Militarization of Indian Country.* East Lansing: Michigan State University Press, 2013.

Lahti, Janne. *Cultural Construction of Empire: The U.S. Army in Arizona and New Mexico.* Lincoln: University of Nebraska Press, 2012.

Langellier, John P. *American Indians in the U.S. Armed Forces, 1866–1945.* Mechanicsburg, PA: Stackpole Books, 2000.

Leckie, William H. *The Buffalo Soldiers: A Narrative of the Negro Cavalry in the West.* Norman: University of Oklahoma Press, 1967.

Linford, Laurance D. *Navajo Places: History, Legend, Landscape.* Salt Lake City: University of Utah Press, 2000.

Link, Martin A., ed. *Navajo: A Century of Progress, 1868–1968.* Window Rock, AZ: Navajo Tribe, 1968.

Lomeli, Francisco, Victor Sorell and Genaro Padilla. *Nuevomexicano Cultural Legacy Forms, Agencies and Discourse.* Albuquerque: University of New Mexico Press, 2002.

MacArthur, Douglas. *Reminiscences.* New York: McGraw Hill, 1964.

Malone, John. "On the Trail of Geronimo." In *Navajo Historical Selections.* Edited by Robert W. Young and Willian Morgan. Phoenix, AZ: Phoenix Indian School Print Shop, 1954.

McNitt, Frank. *The Indian Traders.* Norman: University of Oklahoma Press, 1962.

McPherson, Robert S. *Navajo Land, Navajo Culture: The Utah Experience in the Twentieth Century.* Norman: University of Oklahoma Press, 2001.

Melzer, Richard, and John Taylor. *Tragic Trails and Enchanted Journeys: More Tales of the Rio Abajo.* Los Ranchos, NM: Rio Grande Books, 2017.

Michaelis, Bernhard. *The Navajo Treaty of 1868.* Flagstaff, AZ: Native Child Dinetah, 2014.

Michno, Gregory F. *Encyclopedia of Indian Wars: Western Battles and Skirmishes, 1850–1890.* Missoula, MT: Mountain Press, 2003.

Mitchell, Frank. *Navajo Blessingway Singer: The Autobiography of Frank Mitchell, 1881–1967.* Edited by Charlotte J. Frisbie. Albuquerque: University of New Mexico Press, 1978.

Bibliography

Moore, William Haas. *Chiefs, Agents and Soldiers: Conflict on the Navajo Frontier, 1868–1882.* Albuquerque: University of New Mexico Press, 1994.

Nichols, David A. *Lincoln and the Indians: Civil War Policy and Politics.* Urbana: University of Illinois Press, 2000.

Nolan, Frederick. *The Lincoln County War.* Rev. ed. Santa Fe, NM: Sunstone, 2009.

Oakes, Maud. *Where the Two Came to Their Father: A Navajo War Ceremonial.* New York: Pantheon Books, 1943.

Pershing, John J. *My Life Before the World War, 1860–1917: A Memoir.* Edited by John T. Greenwood. Lexington: University of Kentucky Press, 2013.

Powell, Allan Kent. *San Juan County: People, Resources, and History.* Salt Lake City: Utah State Historical Society, 1983.

Richardson, Gladwell. *Navajo Trader.* Tucson: University of Arizona Press, 2003.

Riley, Glenda. *Confronting Race: Women and Indians on the Frontier, 1815–1915.* Albuquerque: University of New Mexico Press, 2004.

Robinson, Sherry. *Apache Voices: Their Stories of Survival as Told to Eve Ball.* Albuquerque: University of New Mexico Press, 2000.

———. *El Malpais, Mt. Taylor, and the Zuni Mountains.* Albuquerque: University of New Mexico Press, 1994.

———. *I Fought a Good Fight: A History of the Lipan Apaches.* Denton: University of North Texas Press, 2013.

Roessel, Ruth. *Navajo Stories of the Long Walk Period.* Chinle, AZ: Navajo Community College Press, 1973.

Shapard, Bud. *Chief Loco: Apache Peacemaker.* Norman: University of Oklahoma Press, 2010.

Shaw, Harley G., ed. *River of Spirits: A Natural History of New Mexico's Las Animas Creek.* Charleston, SC: The History Press, 2017.

Sheridan, Thomas E. *Arizona: A History.* Rev. ed. Tucson: University of Arizona Press, 2012.

Smitts, David D. "Indian Scouts and Indian Allies in the Frontier Army." In *Major Problems in American Indian History.* Edited by Albert L. Hurtado and Peter Iverson. New York: Houghton Mifflin Company, 2001.

Spicer, Edward H. *Cycles of Conquest: The Impact of Spain, Mexico, and the United States on the Indians of the Southwest, 1533–1960.* Tucson: University of Arizona Press, 1962.

Sweeney, Edwin R. *From Cochise to Geronimo: The Chiricahua Apaches, 1874–1886.* Norman: University of Oklahoma Press, 2010.

Stout, Joseph A., Jr. *Apache Lightning: The Last Great Battle of the Ojo Calientes.* New York: Oxford University Press, 1974.

Taylor, John Lewis. *Looking for Dan: The Puzzling Life of a Frontier Character, Daniel DuBois.* Indianapolis, IN: Dog Ear Publishing, 2014.

Bibliography

Terrell, John Upton. *Apache Chronicle*. New York: World Publishing, 1972.

Thompson, Jerry D. *A Civil War History of the New Mexico Volunteers and Militia*. Albuquerque: University of New Mexico Press, 2015.

———. *Desert Tiger: Captain Paddy Graydon and the Civil War in the Far Southwest*. El Paso: University of Texas at El Paso, 1992.

Thrapp, Dan L. *Al Sieber, Chief of Scouts*. Norman: University of Oklahoma Press, 1964.

———. *Dan Victorio and the Mimbres Apaches*. Norman: University of Oklahoma Press, 1974.

———. *Juh: An Incredible Indian*. El Paso: Texas Western Press, 1973.

Tietjen, Geraldine. *Ramah: A Documentary History, 1920–1925*. Bountiful, UT: Family History Publishers, 1995.

Tiller, Veronica V. *The Jicarilla Apache Tribe: A History*. Lincoln: University of Nebraska Press, 1983.

Tohe, Laura. *Code Talker Stories*. Tucson, AZ: Rio Nuevo Publishers, 2012.

Tyler, Lyman S. *A History of Indian Policy*. Washington, D.C.: United States Printing Office, 1973.

Underhill, Ruth. *Here Come the Navajo!* Lawrence, KS: Haskell Indian Institute, 1953.

Utley, Robert M., and Wilcomb E. Washburn. *American Heritage History of the Indian Wars*. New York: American Heritage Press, 2002.

Viola, Herman J. *Warriors in Uniform: The Legacy of American Indian Heroism*. Washington, D.C.: National Geographic, 2008.

Waters, Frank. *Book of the Hopi*. New York: Viking Press, 1963.

Watt, Robert N. *Apache Tactics, 1830–86*. Oxford, UK: Osprey Publishing, 2012.

Wellman, Paul I. *Death in the Desert: The Fifty Years' War for the Great Southwest*. Lincoln: University of Nebraska Press, 1987. First printing, 1935.

———. *The Indian Wars of the West*. New York: Doubleday, 1954. First printing, 1934.

Wetherill, Louisa Wade, and Harvey Leake. *Wolfkiller: Wisdom from a Nineteenth-Century Navajo Shepherd*. Salt Lake City, UT: Gibbs Smith, 2007.

Wetherill, Marietta. *Life with the Navajos in Chaco Canyon*. Edited by Kathryn Gabreil. Albuquerque: University of New Mexico Press, 1992.

Wheeler, Keith. *The Scouts*. Edited by Jim Hicks. The Old West Series. Alexandria, VA: Time-Life Books, 1978.

Wooster, Robert. *The Military and United States Indian Policy, 1865–1903*. Lincoln: University of Nebraska Press, 1988.

Young, Robert W., and William Morgan. *The Navajo Language*. Salt Lake City, UT: Deseret Book Company, 1871.

Zolbrod, Paul G. *Diné Bahané: The Navajo Creation Story*. Albuquerque: University of New Mexico Press, 1984.

Periodicals

Banks, Leo W. "John Daw, the Navajo 'Big Policeman.'" *Arizona Highways* (February 2003).

Bibo, Arthur. "The Ballad of Placida Romero." Edited by A.E. Roland. *New Mexico Historical Review* (Summer, 2011).

Boelter, Homer H. "Old Navajo Scouts." *The Branding Iron*. Los Angeles Westerners (September 1950).

Carriker, Robert C., and Thompson McFadden. "Thompson McFadden's Diary of an Indian Campaign, 1874." *Southwestern Historical Quarterly* 75, no. 2 (October 1971).

Denetdale, Jennifer Nez. "Securing Navajo National Boundaries, Patriotism, Tradition, and the Diné Marriage Act 2005." *Wicazo Sa Review* 24, no. 2 (Fall 2009): 131–48. JSTOR, http://www.jistor.org?stable/40587784.

Fort Hauchuca Illustrated 7. "Apache Scouts" (1999): 16. http://huachuca.www.army.mil.

Hauptman, Laurence M. "Cadet David Moniac: A Creek Indian's Schooling at West Point, 1817–1822." *Proceedings of the American Philosophical Society* (September 2008).

Hehren, Lawrence L. "Scouting for Mescaleros: The Price Campaign of 1873." *Arizona and the West* 10, no. 2 (Summer 1968): 171–90. JSTOR, http://www.jstor.org/page/info/about/policies/terms.jsp.

Jones, Oakah L., Jr. "The Origins of the Navajo Police, 1872–1873." *Arizona and the West* 8, no. 3 (Autumn 1966). JSTOR, http// www.jstor.org/stable/40167223.

Kelley, Klara, and Harris Francis. "Few Improvements: 'Americans' Challenge Navajos on the Transcontinental Railroad Grant, Arizona, 1881–1887." *American Indian Culture and Research Journal* 25, no. 3 (2001).

Largent, Floyd B., Jr. "Iroquois Chief and Union Officer." *America's Civil War* (June 12, 2006). http://www.historynet.com.

Lekson, Stephen H. "Nana's Raid: Apache Warfare in Southern New Mexico, 1881." *Southwest Studies*, no. 81 (1987).

Lyon, William H. "American and Other Aliens in the Navajo Imagination in the Nineteenth Century." *American Indian Quarterly* 24, no. 1 (Winter 2000).

Manolescu, Kathleen, ed. "Jeff King, Scout, Healer, Councilman." *Leading the Way: The Wisdom of the Navajo People* 14, no. 6 (June 2016).

Riseman, Noah Jed. "Regardless of History?: Re-Assessing the Navajo Codetalkers of World War II." *Australasian Journal of American Studies* 26, no. 2 (December 2007).

Tate, Michael L. "Apache Companies in the US Army, 1891–1897." *Arizona and the West* 16, no. 4 (Winter 1974).

Turcheneske, John A., Jr. "Arizona Press and Geronimo's Surrender." *Journal of Arizona History* 14, no. 2 (Summer 1973): 133–48.
Utley, Robert M. "Victorio's War." *Military History Quarterly* (Autumn 2008).
Watt, Robert N. "'Horses Worn to Mere Shadows': The Ninth U.S. Cavalry's Campaign Against the Apaches in New Mexico Territory, 1879–1881." *New Mexico Historical Review* 86, no. 2 (Spring 2011).
Willie, Eric. "Changing Woman & the Sun: Coming to an Understanding About Setting Up a Home." *Leading the Way: The Wisdom of the Navajo People* 16, no. 8 (August 2018).

Unpublished Works

Carroll, Terry Lee. "Gallup and Her Ceremonial." PhD diss., University of New Mexico, 1971.
Collman, Robert Christie. "Navajo Scouts, 1873–1895: An Integration of Various Cultural Interpretations of Events." Master's thesis, Franconia College, May 1975. Collection of Octavia Fellin Public Library, Gallup, New Mexico, 1975.
Junker, Cecelia B. "Establishment of a Community." Term paper, University of New Mexico–Gallup, 1973. Collection of Octavia Fellin Public Library, Gallup, New Mexico, 1975.
Mason, Joyce Evelyn. "The Use of Indian Scouts in the Apache Wars, 1870–1886." PhD diss., Indiana University, 1970.
Stacher, Herbert C. "History of Crownpoint, New Mexico, 1910–1935: While Samuel Franklin Stacher Was in Charge as Superintendent." Collection of Octavia Fellin Public Library, Gallup, New Mexico, 1986.
Stacher, Samuel Franklin. "Recollections: An Autobiography from the Historical Writings of Samuel Franklin Stacher, 1875–1952." Collected by Herbert C. Stacher. Collection of Octavia Fellin Public Library, Gallup, New Mexico, 1982.
Telling, Irving. "A Social History of the Gallup Area, 1881–1901." PhD diss., Harvard University, 1952.
Tietjen, Gary L. "Encounter with the Frontier." Collection of Octavia Fellin Public Library, Gallup, New Mexico, 1969.
Walker, James C. "From Scouts to Soldiers: The Evolution of Indian Roles in the US Military, 1860–1945." PhD diss., Georgia Southern University, Electronic Thesis and Dissertations Paper, 2013. http://digitalcommons.georgiasouthern.edu/etd.
Zimmerman, E.W., and Pauline Zimmerman. "Our Story on the Trials and Tribulations of Adjusting to the Wild West." Collection of Octavia Fellin Public Library, Gallup, New Mexico.

Bibliography

Newspapers

Arizona Citizen. "Particulars of the Fight on the Animas." October 4, 1879. Chronicling America: Historic American Newspapers, http://chronicilingamerica.gov.

Arizona Sentinel. "General Crook to Enlist 200 Navajo Indian Scouts for the Apache War." November 14, 1885. Chronicling America: Historic American Newspapers, Library of Congress, http://chronicilingamerica.gov.

Arizona Weekly Citizen. "Capture of Geronimo." September 4, 1886. Chronicling America: Historic American Newspapers, Library of Congress, http://chronicilingamerica.gov.

Black Range (NM) Chloride. "Navajo Scouts in Foot Race." August 18, 1886. Chronicling America: Historic American Newspapers, Library of Congress, http://chronicilingamerica.gov.

Brunt, Charles. "Historian: 2 Navajo Women May Have Been First GI Jane." *Gallup Independent*, November 12, 2016.

Correll, J. Lee. "John Daw, Last of the Navajo Scouts." *Navajo Times*, June 24, 1965.

Donovan, Bill. "Diné Scout Lies Buried at Arlington." *Navajo Times*, January 22, 2007.

East Oregonian. "Indian Trader Escapes." September 10, 1921. Chronicling America: Historic American Newspapers, Library of Congress, http://chroniclingamerica.loc.gov.

Gallup Independent. Remarks from Peter Zah, former Navajo president. June 6, 2018.

Las Vegas (NM) Gazette. "Territorial News: Navajo Scouts Refuse to Advance." January 8, 1886. Chronicling America: Historic American Newspapers, http://chronicilingamerica.gov.

Santa Fe New Mexican. "U.S. Attorney, A.G. Pollock Has Special Agent Lowe Investigate Liquor Sale to Navajo Indian Scouts at Ft. Wingate." February 23, 1909. Chronicling America: Historic American Newspapers, Library of Congress, http://chronicilingamerica.gov.

Volkert, Vida. "Oral Navajo History, Culture Preserved on Reel-to-Reel Tape." *Gallup Independent*, June 23, 2018.

Yurth, Cindy. "Manuelito's Legacy." *Navajo Times*, February 14, 2013.

Interviews

Apache, Frank. "Navajo War: Interview with Tom Ration." UNM-Center for Southwest Research, Tape 352, February 1969.

Bibliography

Hauzous, Sam. "Personal Reminiscences Concerning Geronimo: The Warm Springs Apaches and Incidents Surrounding the Submission of Southwestern Apaches." Norman: University of Oklahoma Western History Collection, Tape 194. Transcribed by Linda Butler, 1956.

Manuelito, Bob. "Navajo Scouts: Interview with Tom Ration." UNM-Center for Southwest Research, Tape 345. American Indian Oral History Collection, 1967–72.

Government Documents

U.S. Bureau of Indian Affairs. *Annual Report of the Commissioner of Indian Affairs to the Secretary of the Interior*, 1872.

U.S. Senate Committee on Indian Affairs. *Survey of Conditions of the Indians in the United States*, 14, 33–34.

Online Sources

Arizona Civil War Council. http://www.arizonacivilwarcouncilinc.com.

Ballinger, Gene. "Victorio's War: A Closer Look, Ambush in Massacre Canyon." Buffalo Soldiers & Indian Wars, June 3, 2016. http://www.buffalosoldier.net/BuffaloSoldiers&ChiefVictorio.htm.

Bower, David. "Massacre in Las Animas Canyon Led to End of Apache Victorio." So Far from Heaven. http://www.sofarfromheaven.com.

Carlisle Indian School Digital Resource Center. http://carlisleindian.dickinson.edu.

Find a Grave. "Jose Chavez." https://www.findagrave.com/memorial/3864989/josechavez.

Fisher, Joy. "Baldwin, Frank Dwight." Denver County, Colorado Archives Biographies, August 8, 2009. http://files.usgwarchives.net/co/denver/bios/baldwin297nbs.text.

Holiday, Lindsay F. "American Indian and Alaska Native Veterans: Lasting Contributions." U.S. Department of Veterans Affairs, December 26, 1915. http://www.dod.mil/specials/nativeamerican01.

Lapahie, Harrison, Jr. January 10, 2014. http://www.lapahhic.com/francisco.efm.

Navajo Code Talkers. "Sharing the Story of the Soldiers that Ended the War." Online interviews with thirty-three Navajo Code Talkers, January 27, 2016. http://www.navajocodetalkers.org.

The New Buffalo Soldiers. "Army Reorganization Act of 1866." December 12, 2015. http://www.abuffalosoldier.com.

Second Annual Veterans Summit in Gallup, New Mexico, October 12–13, 2016. Eventbrite. http://eventbrite.com.
Tracking Nana. "Ambush in Gavilan Canyon." http://www.trackingnana.com.
Wikipedia. "Donald McIntosh, September 4, 1834–June 25, 1876." https://en.wikipedian.org/wiki.Donald_McIntosh.
———. "A Guide to the Study of History at Fort Hauchuca, Apache Scouts."
———. "*Rio Grande* (film)." https://en.wikipedia.org/wiki/Rio_Grande_(film).

Film and Television

Defending the Fire. Silver Bullet Productions, 2017.
Geronimo and the Apache Resistance. DVD. Dir. Neil Goodwin. "American Experience," 2007.
Rio Grande. Dir. John Ford. Republic Pictures, November 15, 1950.

About the Author

Photo by John Van't Land.

John Lewis Taylor is a longtime educator in western New Mexico, having served as a teacher and principal for the Bureau of Indian Affairs and as an instructor at the University of New Mexico–Gallup.

John is fascinated with the history of the American Southwest and the Navajo people's role in this drama. The period from the Navajos' return from Fort Sumner in 1868 to the early twentieth century (circa 1917) was an era when the Navajos developed their relationships with the U.S. government. During this time, the modern Navajo Nation was forged. This book explores the beginnings of the Navajos' role with the U.S. military.

John Lewis Taylor holds a Bachelor of Arts in history from Western Kentucky University and a Master of Arts in education from the University of New Mexico. He currently lives with his wife, Betty, in Gallup, New Mexico. He is the author of *Looking for Dan: The Puzzling Life of a Frontier Character Daniel, Dubois*—the biography of a fellow Navajo in-law.

Visit us at
www.historypress.com

www.ingramcontent.com/pod-product-compliance
Lightning Source LLC
Chambersburg PA
CBHW042140160426

43201CB00021B/2356